YOUR BODY WANT TO HEAL- IT JUST NEEDS THE RIGHT INGREDIENTS

HOW FOOD CAN CALM PAIN, SOOTHE YOUR GUT, AND RESTORE YOUR ENERGY

LAUREL K. WYNN

CONTENTS

INTRODUCTION 4

CHAPTER 1: Your Unique Inflammatory Fingerprint 10

CHAPTER 2: The Gut-Brain-Inflammation Axis 18

CHAPTER 3: Beyond Omega-3s: The Complete Anti-Inflammatory Nutrient Matrix 30

CHAPTER 4: Biohacking Your Anti-Inflammatory Response 39

CHAPTER 5: Environmental Factors That Sabotage Progress 49

Smoothies & Elixirs (Pages 59-68)
- Adaptogenic Stress-Relief Smoothie (64)
- Beet Liver Detox Elixir (65)
- Collagen Repair Smoothie (66)
- Ginger Digestive Fire Elixir (63)
- Golden Turmeric Smoothie (59)
- Green Powerhouse (60)
- Hibiscus Antioxidant Elixir (67)
- Matcha Green Tea Recovery Smoothie (68)
- Omega-3 Brain Boost Smoothie (62)
- Tart Cherry Anti-Pain Elixir (61)

Breakfast Bowls (Pages 70-84)
- Antioxidant Acai Bowl (78)
- Berry Yogurt Bowl (73)
- Coconut Curry Breakfast Bowl (77)
- Golden Turmeric Quinoa Power Bowl (70)
- Green Goddess Avocado Bowl (72)
- Mediterranean Herb Bowl (76)
- Omega-3 Chia Seed Pudding Bowl (71)
- Protein-Packed Quinoa Breakfast Bowl (75)
- Protein-Rich Lentil Bowl (81)
- Savory Egg and Vegetable Bowl (83)
- Savory Mushroom and Herb Bowl (79)
- Spiced Apple Cinnamon Bowl (82)
- Warming Ginger Oat Bowl (74)
- Warming Golden Milk Bowl (84)
- Warming Sweet Potato Hash Bowl (80)

Healing Soups & Broths (Pages 86-95)
- Beet and Ginger Borscht (93)
- Ginger-Garlic Immune Support Broth (88)
- Golden Bone Broth with Turmeric and Ginger (86)
- Gut-Healing Cabbage and Ginger Soup (92)
- Healing Chicken and Vegetable Soup (91)
- Healing Fish and Fennel Broth (94)
- Mushroom-Miso Adaptogenic Broth (90)
- Spiced Sweet Potato and Coconut Soup (95)
- Turmeric Lentil Healing Soup (89)
- Vegetable Miso Soup (87)

Fermented Foods (Pages 97-106)
- Cultured Butter and Buttermilk (106)
- Cultured Cashew Cheese (102)
- Fermented Garlic Honey (105)
- Fermented Hot Sauce (103)
- Fermented Salsa Verde (100)
- Ginger-Carrot Kvass Digestive Tonic (98)
- Probiotic Beet Kvass (104)
- Probiotic Coconut Yogurt (99)
- Traditional Water Kefir (101)
- Turmeric Kraut (97)

Snacks and Treats (Pages 108-117)
- Chocolate Bark (110)
- Coconut Matcha Fat Bombs (112)
- Ginger-Turmeric Gummies (114)
- Golden Turmeric Energy Balls (108)
- Omega-3 Seed Crackers (109)
- Probiotic Coconut Yogurt Parfait Cups (117)
- Savory Herb and Seed Bites (115)
- Spiced Sweet Potato Chips (111)
- Trail Mix (113)

INTRODUCTION

Your body is fighting a war you cannot see. Right now, as you read these words, microscopic battles are raging throughout your system. The question is not whether inflammation is present in your body—it is whether this inflammation is working for you or against you.

THE TWO FACES OF INFLAMMATION: YOUR BODY'S JEKYLL AND HYDE RESPONSE

Inflammation represents one of your body's most sophisticated defense mechanisms, yet it has become your greatest enemy in the modern world. To understand how to harness this powerful system, you must first recognize that inflammation operates in two distinct modes: acute protective inflammation and chronic destructive inflammation.

Acute Protective Inflammation: Your Body's Emergency Response Team

When you cut your finger, twist your ankle, or encounter a bacterial infection, your body launches an immediate, coordinated response. This acute inflammation represents a marvel of biological engineering. Within seconds of tissue damage, specialized cells release chemical signals that trigger a cascade of protective actions.

Blood vessels dilate to increase blood flow to the affected area, delivering essential immune cells and nutrients needed for repair. Capillary walls become more permeable, allowing white blood cells to exit the bloodstream and enter tissues where they can neutralize threats and remove damaged cells. This process creates the familiar signs of acute inflammation: redness, swelling, heat, and pain.

The remarkable aspect of acute inflammation lies in its self-limiting nature. Once the threat has been neutralized and healing begins, your body activates specialized resolution pathways that actively turn off the inflammatory response. Anti-inflammatory mediators are released, immune cells are cleared away, and tissues return to their normal state. This entire process typically resolves within hours to days.

Chronic Destructive Inflammation: When Your Defense System Turns Against You

Chronic inflammation represents acute inflammation's dangerous twin. Instead of resolving after completing its protective mission, chronic inflammation persists for months or years, creating a state of continuous tissue damage and repair that ultimately overwhelms your body's healing capacity.

Unlike acute inflammation, which you can feel and identify, chronic inflammation operates silently beneath your awareness. You will not experience the obvious signs of redness, swelling, or localized pain. Instead, chronic inflammation manifests as subtle, systemic changes that gradually erode your health over time.

The cellular environment during chronic inflammation becomes toxic. Immune cells that should protect you begin releasing damaging chemicals continuously. Free radicals accumulate faster than your antioxidant systems can neutralize them. Tissues become increasingly damaged, and your body's repair mechanisms become overwhelmed and dysfunctional.

This process creates a vicious cycle. Damaged tissues trigger more inflammation, which causes more damage, which triggers more inflammation. Your body becomes trapped in a state of perpetual internal conflict, gradually destroying the very tissues it seeks to protect.

The Modern Perfect Storm: How Your Lifestyle Fuels Chronic Inflammation

Your ancestors lived in a world where acute inflammation served them well. Cuts, infections, and injuries required immediate, powerful responses to ensure survival. However, chronic inflammation was relatively rare because the environmental triggers that sustain it were largely absent from their daily lives.

Today, you face an unprecedented combination of inflammatory triggers that create what researchers call the "perfect storm" for chronic inflammation. These triggers assault your system continuously, never allowing your inflammatory response to resolve naturally.

The Dietary Disaster: How Modern Food Ignites Inflammation

Your standard modern diet represents a fundamental mismatch with your body's evolutionary programming. Processed foods, refined sugars, and industrial oils create a constant state of metabolic inflammation that your body cannot resolve.

When you consume foods high in refined carbohydrates, your blood sugar spikes rapidly, triggering the release of inflammatory mediators. Your body perceives these sudden glucose elevations as a threat, mounting an inflammatory response to protect your tissues from damage. However, because you likely consume these foods multiple times daily, your inflammatory system never has the opportunity to stand down.

Industrial seed oils, which now comprise nearly 20 percent of your total caloric intake, contain inflammatory omega-6 fatty acids in concentrations that would have been impossible to achieve through natural foods. These oils become incorporated into your cell membranes, making every cell in your body more susceptible to inflammatory damage.

Processed foods contain additives, preservatives, and artificial ingredients that your immune system recognizes as foreign substances. Your body mounts an inflammatory response to these chemicals, treating them as invaders that must be neutralized. The constant exposure to these substances keeps your immune system in a perpetual state of high alert.

The Stress Epidemic: How Your Mind Inflames Your Body

Chronic psychological stress represents one of the most powerful drivers of systemic inflammation. When you experience stress, your body releases cortisol and other stress hormones designed to help you cope with immediate threats. However, the chronic stress of modern life—financial pressures, work demands, relationship conflicts, and information overload—keeps these stress systems activated continuously.

Chronic stress disrupts your body's natural circadian rhythms, interfering with the timing of anti-inflammatory processes that normally occur during sleep and rest periods. Your stress response system becomes dysregulated, alternating between states of excessive cortisol production and cortisol resistance, both of which promote inflammation.

The psychological impact of chronic stress also drives behavioral changes that further fuel inflammation. Stress often leads to poor food choices, disrupted sleep patterns, reduced physical activity, and increased consumption of alcohol or other inflammatory substances.

The Sleep Deprivation Crisis: When Rest Becomes Inflammatory

Sleep represents your body's primary opportunity to activate anti-inflammatory and repair processes. During deep sleep, your brain's glymphatic system clears inflammatory waste products, your immune system resets, and your body produces growth hormone and other healing compounds.

However, modern lifestyle factors conspire to disrupt your sleep quality and duration. Artificial light exposure, particularly blue light from electronic devices, suppresses melatonin production and delays sleep onset. Caffeine consumption, irregular meal timing, and high stress levels further interfere with natural sleep patterns.

Sleep deprivation creates a state of chronic low-grade inflammation that affects every system in your body. Even a single night of poor sleep increases inflammatory markers measurably, and chronic sleep disruption creates persistent inflammatory activation that becomes increasingly difficult to resolve.

The Sedentary Trap: How Inactivity Ignites Inflammation

Your body evolved for regular movement and physical activity. However, modern life often involves prolonged periods of sitting, minimal physical exertion, and limited exposure to natural environments. This sedentary lifestyle creates multiple pathways to chronic inflammation.

Physical inactivity leads to poor circulation, which impairs the delivery of oxygen and nutrients to tissues while allowing inflammatory waste products to accumulate. Muscles that remain inactive for extended periods begin to atrophy and release inflammatory chemicals. Your cardiovascular system becomes less efficient, creating conditions that promote inflammatory damage to blood vessels.

Regular movement, particularly activities that engage large muscle groups, stimulates the production of anti-inflammatory compounds and helps maintain healthy circulation. The absence of this regular anti-inflammatory stimulus allows chronic inflammation to persist and intensify over time.

Beyond Arthritis and Heart Disease: The Far-Reaching Impact of Chronic Inflammation

Most people associate inflammation with obvious conditions like arthritis or heart disease. However, chronic inflammation affects virtually every organ system in your body, contributing to a vast array of health problems that may seem unrelated to inflammation.

The Brain Under Fire: Neuroinflammation and Mental Health

Your brain contains specialized immune cells called microglia that monitor for threats and damage. When activated by chronic inflammation, these cells release inflammatory chemicals that damage neurons and disrupt normal brain function.

Neuroinflammation contributes to depression, anxiety, brain fog, memory problems, and cognitive decline. The inflammatory chemicals interfere with neurotransmitter production and signaling, creating imbalances that affect mood, motivation, and mental clarity. This connection explains why people with chronic inflammatory conditions often experience mental health challenges alongside their physical symptoms.

The Digestive System: Where Inflammation Begins and Spreads

Your digestive tract houses approximately 70 percent of your immune system, making it both a common source of inflammation and a critical target for anti-inflammatory interventions. Chronic inflammation in the gut disrupts the intestinal barrier, allowing partially digested food particles, toxins, and bacteria to enter your bloodstream.

This condition, known as increased intestinal permeability or "leaky gut," triggers systemic inflammation as your immune system responds to these foreign substances. The resulting inflammation can manifest as digestive symptoms, skin problems, autoimmune reactions, and widespread systemic symptoms that seem unrelated to digestive health.

The Metabolic Consequence: How Inflammation Drives Weight Gain and Diabetes

Chronic inflammation directly interferes with your body's ability to regulate blood sugar and maintain healthy weight. Inflammatory chemicals disrupt insulin signaling, making your cells less responsive to insulin and promoting fat storage, particularly around your midsection.

This metabolic dysfunction creates a vicious cycle where inflammation promotes weight gain, and excess weight, particularly visceral fat, produces more inflammatory chemicals. The result is a self-perpetuating cycle of inflammation, insulin resistance, and metabolic dysfunction that becomes increasingly difficult to break without targeted intervention.

The Hormonal Disruption: Inflammation's Impact on Endocrine Function

Your endocrine system relies on precise chemical signaling to maintain hormonal balance. Chronic inflammation disrupts this delicate system, interfering with the production, transport, and utilization of hormones throughout your body.

Inflammatory chemicals can bind to hormone receptors, blocking normal hormone action. They can also increase the production of stress hormones while suppressing the production of beneficial hormones like growth hormone and sex hormones. This hormonal disruption affects energy levels, mood, reproductive function, and overall vitality.

ASSESSING YOUR PERSONAL INFLAMMATORY PROFILE

Understanding your individual inflammatory status requires a combination of symptom recognition, lifestyle assessment, and when possible, objective biomarker evaluation. This personal assessment will help you identify your specific inflammatory triggers and monitor your progress as you implement anti-inflammatory strategies.

The Inflammatory Symptom Inventory

Chronic inflammation manifests through a wide range of symptoms that often appear unrelated. Rate each of the following symptoms on a scale of 0-3, where 0 represents never experiencing the symptom, 1 represents occasional occurrence, 2 represents frequent occurrence, and 3 represents constant or severe occurrence.

➢ Physical Symptoms:
- Joint pain, stiffness, or swelling, particularly in the morning
- Muscle aches and pains without apparent cause
- Chronic fatigue that does not improve with rest
- Skin problems including eczema, psoriasis, acne, or unexplained rashes
- Digestive issues such as bloating, gas, diarrhea, or constipation
- Frequent infections or slow healing from minor injuries
- Allergies or increased sensitivity to environmental triggers
- Headaches or migraines that occur regularly
- Sleep disturbances including difficulty falling asleep or staying asleep
- Unexplained weight gain, particularly around the midsection

➢ Cognitive and Emotional Symptoms:
- Brain fog or difficulty concentrating
- Memory problems or forgetfulness
- Mood swings or increased irritability
- Anxiety or feelings of overwhelm
- Depression or persistent low mood
- Lack of motivation or enthusiasm
- Difficulty making decisions
- Increased emotional reactivity to stress

➢ Scoring Your Inflammatory Load:
- 0-10: Low inflammatory burden
- 11-20: Moderate inflammatory burden
- 21-30: High inflammatory burden
- Above 30: Severe inflammatory burden requiring immediate attention

Lifestyle Inflammatory Risk Assessment

Your daily habits and environmental exposures significantly influence your inflammatory status. Evaluate each of the following categories to identify areas where lifestyle modifications could reduce your inflammatory burden.

➢ Dietary Assessment:
- Frequency of processed food consumption
- Added sugar intake from beverages, snacks, and desserts
- Consumption of refined grains and flour-based products
- Intake of industrial seed oils and fried foods
- Alcohol consumption patterns
- Fruit and vegetable intake adequacy
- Quality and variety of protein sources
- Hydration habits and beverage choices

➢ Sleep and Recovery Assessment:

- Average sleep duration and consistency
- Sleep quality and morning energy levels
- Evening screen time and light exposure
- Bedroom environment optimization
- Stress levels at bedtime
- Recovery time needed from physical or mental exertion

➤ Stress and Mental Health Assessment:
- Chronic stress levels from work, relationships, or finances
- Coping strategies and stress management techniques
- Social support systems and relationship quality
- Work-life balance and time management
- Exposure to environmental stressors
- Mental health history and current status

➤ Physical Activity and Movement Assessment:
- Daily movement patterns and sedentary time
- Structured exercise frequency and intensity
- Recovery time needed between exercise sessions
- Enjoyment and sustainability of current activity levels
- Outdoor time and nature exposure
- Flexibility and mobility practices

Understanding Basic Inflammatory Biomarkers

While symptoms and lifestyle factors provide valuable insights into your inflammatory status, objective biomarkers offer additional information about your body's inflammatory processes. These tests can help you monitor progress and identify specific areas that require attention.

C - reactive protein (CRP) and High-Sensitivity CRP (hs-CRP)

C-reactive protein represents the most commonly measured inflammatory marker. Your liver produces CRP in response to inflammatory signals, and elevated levels indicate the presence of systemic inflammation. High-sensitivity CRP can detect lower levels of inflammation and provides more precise information about cardiovascular risk.

Optimal hs-CRP levels fall below 1.0 mg/L, with levels between 1.0-3.0 mg/L indicating moderate risk and levels above 3.0 mg/L suggesting high inflammatory burden. However, these values represent population averages, and your optimal level may be lower than the standard reference ranges.

Erythrocyte Sedimentation Rate (ESR)

ESR measures how quickly red blood cells settle in a test tube over one hour. Elevated ESR indicates the presence of inflammatory proteins in your blood that cause red blood cells to clump together and settle more rapidly. While less specific than CRP, ESR provides complementary information about inflammatory activity.

Fasting Insulin and Glucose

Metabolic markers like fasting insulin and glucose provide insights into metabolic inflammation. Elevated fasting insulin levels often precede elevated glucose levels and indicate insulin resistance, which both causes and results from chronic inflammation. Optimal fasting insulin levels should be below 5 mIU/L, with levels above 10 mIU/L indicating significant metabolic dysfunction.

Omega-3 Index

The omega-3 index measures the percentage of EPA and DHA in your red blood cell membranes, providing information about your anti-inflammatory fatty acid status. An optimal omega-3 index should exceed 8 percent, with levels below 4 percent indicating significant deficiency in these anti-inflammatory compounds.

Homocysteine

Elevated homocysteine levels indicate inflammation and oxidative stress, particularly in the cardiovascular system. Optimal homocysteine levels should be below 7 µmol/L, with levels above 10 µmol/L indicating increased inflammatory burden and potential nutrient deficiencies.

Vitamin D

Vitamin D functions as both a hormone and an anti-inflammatory compound. Deficiency in vitamin D contributes to increased inflammatory activity and impaired immune function. Optimal vitamin D levels should be between 40-80 ng/mL (100-200 nmol/L), with levels below 30 ng/mL indicating deficiency.

Taking Action: Your Next Steps

Your journey toward reducing chronic inflammation begins with honest self-assessment and commitment to systematic change. The inflammatory assessment tools provided in this chapter will help you identify your current status and track your progress as you implement the strategies outlined in subsequent chapters.

Start by completing the symptom inventory and lifestyle assessment. This baseline evaluation will help you identify your primary inflammatory triggers and the areas where you have the greatest opportunity for improvement. Consider having your inflammatory biomarkers tested to provide objective data about your current status.

Remember that chronic inflammation developed over months or years, and reversing it requires patience and consistency. However, many people begin to notice improvements in energy, mood, and physical symptoms within weeks of implementing targeted anti-inflammatory strategies.

The following chapters will provide you with the specific tools and strategies needed to address each aspect of your inflammatory profile. By understanding your unique inflammatory fingerprint and implementing personalized interventions, you can begin to restore balance to your body's inflammatory systems and reclaim your health and vitality.

Chapter 1

Your Unique Inflammatory Fingerprint

No two people respond to inflammation in exactly the same way. While the fundamental mechanisms of inflammation remain consistent across all humans, your individual response pattern—your inflammatory fingerprint—is as unique as your actual fingerprint. Understanding this personal pattern is crucial for developing an effective anti-inflammatory strategy that works specifically for your body.

Your inflammatory fingerprint is shaped by four primary factors: your genetic makeup, your age and life stage, your biological sex, and your accumulated exposure to inflammatory triggers throughout your lifetime. By understanding how each of these factors influences your inflammatory response, you can tailor your approach to achieve maximum results with minimum effort.

Decoding Your Genetic Inflammatory Blueprint

Your genes do not determine your destiny, but they do influence how your body responds to inflammatory triggers and how effectively you can resolve inflammation once it begins. The good news is that you can understand your genetic tendencies without expensive genetic testing by observing your body's responses and your family health history.

The Celtic Curse: Iron Accumulation and Inflammation

If you have Northern European ancestry, particularly Irish, Scottish, or Welsh heritage, you may carry genetic variants that cause your body

to absorb and store excess iron. This condition, known as hereditary hemochromatosis, affects approximately 1 in 200 people of Celtic descent, making it one of the most common genetic conditions.

Excess iron acts as a powerful pro-inflammatory agent in your body. Iron catalyzes the formation of reactive oxygen species, which damage tissues and trigger inflammatory responses. Even mild iron overload can contribute to chronic inflammation, particularly affecting your liver, joints, and cardiovascular system.

Identifying Your Iron Status Without Testing:

Look for these family history patterns and personal symptoms that suggest iron accumulation:
- Family history of liver disease, diabetes, heart problems, or arthritis, particularly in men over 40
- Joint pain and stiffness, especially in your hands and knuckles
- Chronic fatigue that doesn't improve with rest
- Skin bronzing or unusual tanning
- Loss of body hair or changes in sexual function
- Family members who were told to avoid iron supplements or to donate blood regularly

Iron Management Strategies:

If you suspect iron accumulation, focus on natural iron regulation through your diet:
- Drink tea or coffee with meals to reduce iron absorption
- Increase your intake of calcium-rich foods, which compete with iron for absorption
- Consume vitamin C separately from iron-rich meals
- Consider regular blood donation if medically appropriate
- Avoid cooking in cast iron cookware
- Limit consumption of iron-fortified foods and supplements containing iron

The Mediterranean Advantage: Enhanced Antioxidant Processing

People with Mediterranean ancestry often carry genetic variants that enhance their ability to process and utilize antioxidant compounds. These genetic advantages evolved in populations with high exposure to intense sunlight and diets rich in polyphenolic compounds from olive oil, wine, and aromatic herbs.

If you have Mediterranean heritage, you may notice that you tolerate sun exposure better than others, have fewer skin problems, and respond particularly well to diets rich in olive oil, herbs, and moderate amounts of red wine. Your genetic makeup likely allows you to extract maximum benefit from polyphenol-rich foods.

Maximizing Your Mediterranean Genetic Advantage:

- Prioritize high-quality extra virgin olive oil as your primary cooking fat
- Include herbs like oregano, rosemary, and thyme daily in your meals
- Consider moderate red wine consumption with meals if alcohol is appropriate for you
- Focus on colorful vegetables and fruits high in anthocyanins and flavonoids
- Include nuts, particularly almonds and walnuts, in your daily routine

The Asian Flush: Acetaldehyde Sensitivity and Inflammation

Approximately 36% of people of East Asian descent carry genetic variants that impair their ability to metabolize alcohol efficiently. This creates a buildup of acetaldehyde, a toxic compound that causes facial flushing, nausea, and headaches after alcohol consumption.

More importantly for inflammation, acetaldehyde is highly inflammatory and contributes to oxidative stress throughout your body. If you experience alcohol flush reaction, even small amounts of alcohol can trigger significant inflammatory responses that may persist for hours after consumption.

Managing Acetaldehyde Sensitivity:

- Avoid or strictly limit alcohol consumption
- If you choose to drink, select beverages with lower congener content like vodka or gin
- Never drink on an empty stomach

- Increase your intake of foods rich in glutathione precursors like cruciferous vegetables
- Consider supplementing with N-acetylcysteine to support acetaldehyde metabolism
- Focus on other sources of antioxidants like green tea instead of relying on red wine

The APOE4 Variant: Enhanced Inflammatory Sensitivity

The APOE4 genetic variant, carried by approximately 25% of the population, influences how your body responds to dietary fats and inflammatory triggers. People with this variant tend to have more pronounced inflammatory responses to saturated fats and may be more sensitive to environmental toxins.

You might carry the APOE4 variant if you have a strong family history of Alzheimer's disease, cardiovascular disease, or if you notice that high-fat meals make you feel sluggish or unwell. People with this variant often feel better on lower-fat, higher-carbohydrate diets than the general population.

APOE4-Friendly Anti-Inflammatory Strategies:

- Emphasize omega-3 rich fish over other animal proteins
- Limit saturated fat intake from red meat and dairy
- Increase your consumption of colorful vegetables and fruits
- Focus on complex carbohydrates from whole grains and legumes
- Prioritize regular exercise, which provides enhanced benefits for APOE4 carriers
- Consider intermittent fasting protocols, which may provide neuroprotective benefits

Family History Pattern Recognition

Your family health history provides valuable clues about your genetic inflammatory tendencies, even without formal genetic testing. Look for patterns across multiple family members, particularly those who share your genetic background.

➢ Cardiovascular Inflammation Patterns:
- Early heart attacks or strokes (before age 65)
- High blood pressure across multiple family members
- Elevated cholesterol despite healthy lifestyles
- Blood clotting disorders or stroke

➢ Autoimmune and Allergic Patterns:
- Multiple family members with different autoimmune conditions
- Seasonal allergies, asthma, or eczema
- Food allergies or sensitivities
- Inflammatory bowel conditions

➢ Metabolic Inflammation Patterns:
- Type 2 diabetes across multiple generations
- Obesity that's difficult to manage despite diet efforts
- Fatty liver disease or elevated liver enzymes
- Gout or elevated uric acid levels

➢ Neuroinflammatory Patterns:
- Depression or anxiety across multiple family members
- Alzheimer's disease or early cognitive decline
- Migraine headaches
- Attention deficit disorders

Understanding these patterns helps you anticipate your vulnerabilities and implement targeted prevention strategies before problems develop.

Age-Related Inflammatory Changes and Adaptation Strategies

Your inflammatory system changes significantly as you age, requiring different strategies at different life stages. Understanding these changes allows you to adapt your anti-inflammatory approach to match your body's evolving needs.

The Inflammatory Decades: Ages 20-40

During your twenties and thirties, your inflammatory system typically functions at peak efficiency. You can recover quickly from acute inflammation, your antioxidant systems work effectively, and your body maintains strong inflammatory resolution pathways.

However, this period often involves lifestyle choices that set the stage for future inflammatory problems. Career stress, irregular eating patterns, decreased physical activity, and social drinking can begin to overwhelm your inflammatory resilience, even if you don't notice immediate consequences.

Optimization Strategies for Young Adults:

Focus on building inflammatory resilience for the future:
- Establish consistent sleep patterns that you can maintain long-term
- Learn stress management techniques before chronic stress becomes overwhelming
- Build muscle mass and cardiovascular fitness to support lifelong health
- Develop cooking skills and healthy eating habits that don't depend on willpower
- Limit alcohol consumption and avoid smoking or recreational drugs
- Address digestive issues early before they become chronic problems

The Transition Years: Ages 40-55

Your forties and fifties represent a critical transition period where inflammatory resilience begins to decline. You may notice that you don't recover from physical exertion as quickly, sleep disturbances become more common, and minor dietary indiscretions cause more pronounced symptoms.

This period often coincides with peak career stress, family responsibilities, and the beginning of hormonal changes. The combination of increased inflammatory triggers and decreased inflammatory resilience creates a perfect storm for the development of chronic inflammatory conditions.

Adaptation Strategies for Midlife:

- Prioritize sleep quality over sleep quantity if you can't achieve both
- Implement more structured stress management practices

- Increase your intake of anti-inflammatory foods while reducing inflammatory triggers
- Focus on maintaining muscle mass through resistance training
- Address hormonal changes proactively through lifestyle and, if appropriate, medical intervention
- Invest in regular health screenings to catch inflammatory conditions early
- Develop sustainable exercise routines that account for longer recovery times

The Wisdom Years: Ages 55 and Beyond

After age 55, your body experiences a phenomenon called "inflammaging"—a chronic, low-grade inflammatory state that contributes to many age-related diseases. Your immune system becomes less efficient at resolving inflammation, and your antioxidant systems require more support to function effectively.

However, this life stage also offers opportunities for optimization. Many people have more time to focus on health, less career stress, and the wisdom to prioritize what truly matters for their wellbeing.

Strategic Approaches for Older Adults:

- Emphasize anti-inflammatory foods and consider targeted supplementation
- Focus on maintaining functional movement rather than peak performance
- Prioritize social connections and mental stimulation to combat neuroinflammation
- Address age-related nutrient absorption issues through food combining and supplementation
- Implement regular detoxification support through diet and lifestyle
- Consider intermittent fasting protocols appropriate for your health status
- Work with healthcare providers who understand the inflammatory basis of age-related diseases

Gender-Specific Inflammatory Patterns and Nutritional Needs

Biological sex significantly influences inflammatory responses and nutritional requirements. Understanding these differences allows you to optimize your anti-inflammatory strategy based on your specific physiological needs.

Women's Inflammatory Patterns

Women experience unique inflammatory challenges related to hormonal fluctuations, reproductive health, and differences in immune system function. Estrogen generally provides anti-inflammatory benefits, while progesterone can be pro-inflammatory. These hormonal fluctuations create cyclical changes in inflammatory status that require adaptive strategies.

Menstrual Cycle Inflammatory Variations:

Your inflammatory status changes predictably throughout your menstrual cycle:
- Days 1-5 (Menstruation): Inflammatory prostaglandins cause cramping and systemic inflammation
- Days 6-14 (Follicular Phase): Rising estrogen provides anti-inflammatory benefits
- Days 15-28 (Luteal Phase): Progesterone dominance can increase inflammatory sensitivity

Cycle-Specific Nutritional Strategies:

➢ During Menstruation:
- Increase omega-3 fatty acids to compete with inflammatory prostaglandins
- Focus on iron-rich foods to replace menstrual losses
- Include magnesium-rich foods to support muscle relaxation
- Consume warming, anti-inflammatory spices like ginger and turmeric

➢ During Follicular Phase:
- Take advantage of improved insulin sensitivity with moderate carbohydrate intake
- Focus on foods that support estrogen metabolism like cruciferous vegetables

- Include plenty of colorful antioxidants to support the antioxidant benefits of estrogen

➢ During Luteal Phase:
- Reduce refined carbohydrates to prevent progesterone-induced insulin resistance
- Increase consumption of calming, anti-inflammatory foods
- Focus on foods rich in B-vitamins to support progesterone metabolism
- Include foods that support serotonin production to counteract mood changes

Pregnancy and Lactation Considerations:

Pregnancy creates unique inflammatory challenges as your immune system must balance protecting you while tolerating the developing baby. Morning sickness, gestational diabetes, and preeclampsia all have inflammatory components.

➢ Anti-Inflammatory Pregnancy Strategies:
- Prioritize omega-3 fatty acids for fetal brain development and maternal mood
- Include folate-rich foods to support proper DNA methylation
- Focus on easily digestible, nutrient-dense foods during morning sickness
- Maintain stable blood sugar to prevent gestational diabetes
- Include probiotic foods to support maternal and infant gut health

Menopause and Hormonal Changes:

The decline in estrogen during menopause removes significant anti-inflammatory protection, often leading to increased inflammatory conditions. Hot flashes, joint pain, mood changes, and increased cardiovascular risk all relate to increased inflammatory activity.

➢ Menopause-Specific Anti-Inflammatory Approaches:
- Increase phytoestrogen-rich foods like flax seeds, sesame seeds, and legumes
- Focus on calcium and magnesium for bone health and mood stability
- Include cooling foods and herbs to manage hot flashes

- Prioritize foods that support liver detoxification of hormones
- Consider intermittent fasting to improve insulin sensitivity and reduce inflammation

Men's Inflammatory Patterns

Men typically experience more consistent inflammatory patterns but face unique challenges related to testosterone levels, cardiovascular health, and different stress responses. Testosterone generally provides anti-inflammatory benefits, but declining levels with age can contribute to increased inflammatory burden.

Age-Related Testosterone Decline:

Men experience gradual testosterone decline beginning around age 30, losing approximately 1% per year. This decline contributes to increased inflammatory activity, particularly affecting muscle mass, energy levels, and cardiovascular health.

➢ Supporting Healthy Testosterone Through Nutrition:
- Include zinc-rich foods like oysters, beef, and pumpkin seeds
- Focus on healthy fats from nuts, avocados, and olive oil
- Consume adequate protein to support muscle mass
- Include cruciferous vegetables to support healthy hormone metabolism
- Limit alcohol consumption, which suppresses testosterone production
- Maintain stable blood sugar to prevent insulin-related hormone disruption

Cardiovascular Inflammatory Focus:

Men develop cardiovascular disease earlier than women, often related to inflammatory damage to blood vessels. This requires particular attention to cardiovascular anti-inflammatory strategies.

➢ Male-Specific Cardiovascular Protection:
- Prioritize omega-3 fatty acids from fish and marine sources

- Include foods rich in nitrates like leafy greens and beets for blood vessel health
- Focus on potassium-rich foods to support healthy blood pressure
- Limit sodium intake from processed foods
- Include antioxidant-rich foods to protect blood vessels from oxidative damage

Stress Response Differences:

Men and women respond differently to stress, with men more likely to experience cardiovascular consequences and women more likely to experience immune system effects. Men benefit from anti-inflammatory strategies that specifically address cardiovascular stress responses.

➢ Male Stress Management Through Nutrition:
- Include magnesium-rich foods to support healthy blood pressure responses
- Focus on B-vitamins to support healthy stress hormone metabolism
- Consume adapogenic herbs like ashwagandha to modulate stress responses
- Include foods that support healthy sleep patterns
- Limit caffeine intake, which can exaggerate stress responses in men

Identifying Your Personal Inflammatory Triggers Through Systematic Elimination

Understanding your genetic tendencies, age-related changes, and gender-specific patterns provides the foundation for identifying your personal inflammatory triggers. However, the most powerful tool for discovering your unique inflammatory fingerprint is systematic elimination and reintroduction of potential triggers.

The Foundation Phase: Establishing Your Baseline

Before you can identify specific triggers, you need to establish a stable, low-inflammatory baseline. This requires removing the most common inflammatory triggers while supporting your body's natural anti-inflammatory systems.

The 21-Day Foundation Protocol:

➢ Week 1: Remove Major Inflammatory Triggers
- Eliminate refined sugars and artificial sweeteners
- Remove processed foods and restaurant meals
- Avoid industrial seed oils and fried foods
- Stop alcohol consumption temporarily
- Remove gluten-containing grains
- Eliminate dairy products
- Avoid nightshade vegetables (tomatoes, peppers, eggplant, and potatoes)

➢ Week 2: Add Anti-Inflammatory Support
- Include omega-3 rich fish 3-4 times per week
- Consume 8-10 servings of colorful vegetables daily
- Add anti-inflammatory spices to every meal
- Include fermented foods daily
- Drink anti-inflammatory teas like green tea and turmeric tea
- Ensure adequate sleep and stress management

➢ Week 3: Stabilize and Assess
- Continue the elimination protocol
- Track your symptoms daily using the assessment tools from Chapter 1
- Note changes in energy, mood, digestion, sleep, and physical symptoms
- Prepare for the systematic reintroduction phase

The Detective Phase: Systematic Reintroduction

After establishing your foundation, you can begin systematically reintroducing potential triggers one at a time. This process requires patience and careful observation, but it provides invaluable information about your personal inflammatory responses.

Reintroduction Protocol Guidelines:

➢ General Rules:
- Reintroduce only one food group at a time
- Allow 3-4 days between reintroductions
- Consume the test food 2-3 times on the first day of reintroduction
- Monitor symptoms for 72 hours after each reintroduction
- If you experience reactions, wait until symptoms resolve before testing the next food

- Keep detailed records of foods tested and reactions experienced

Suggested Reintroduction Order:

1. Non-gluten grains (rice, quinoa, and oats)
   - Start with small portions with meals
   - Watch for digestive symptoms, energy changes, or joint pain
   - White rice is typically the least reactive grain to test first

2. Legumes (beans, lentils, chickpeas)
   - Begin with well-cooked, easily digestible varieties
   - Monitor for digestive symptoms and bloating
   - Soak and cook thoroughly to reduce anti-nutrients

3. Dairy products (start with grass-fed, full-fat options)
   - Test different types separately: butter, cheese, yogurt, milk
   - Watch for digestive symptoms, skin changes, and respiratory symptoms
   - Consider starting with fermented dairy like kefir or yogurt

4. Nightshade vegetables (tomatoes, peppers, eggplant, potatoes)
   - Test each variety separately
   - Monitor for joint pain, skin changes, or digestive symptoms
   - Some people react to specific nightshades but not others

5. Gluten-containing grains (wheat, barley, rye)
   - Start with ancient varieties if available
   - Watch for digestive symptoms, brain fog, mood changes, and joint pain
   - Consider testing different forms (bread vs. pasta vs. beer)

6. Alcohol (if appropriate for your health status)
   - Test different types separately
   - Monitor for sleep disruption, mood changes, and inflammation markers
   - Consider organic, sulfite-free options first

Advanced Trigger Identification

Beyond the common dietary triggers, many people have additional inflammatory sensitivities that require more sophisticated detective work.

Chemical and Environmental Triggers:

- Artificial fragrances and cleaning products
- Food additives and preservatives
- Heavy metals from dental work or environmental exposure
- Mold exposure in living or work environments
- Electromagnetic field exposure from devices and WiFi

Food Additive Investigation:

Common additives that trigger inflammation in sensitive individuals:
- MSG and other glutamates
- Artificial colors and dyes
- Preservatives like BHA, BHT, and sodium benzoate
- Carrageenan in dairy alternatives
- Natural flavors (which can contain multiple chemical compounds)

Hidden Inflammatory Foods:

Some apparently healthy foods can be inflammatory for certain individuals:
- High-histamine foods like aged cheeses, fermented foods, and cured meats
- High-oxalate foods like spinach, almonds, and chocolate
- FODMAPs in sensitive individuals
- Lectins in grains, legumes, and some vegetables
- Salicylates in certain fruits, vegetables, and herbs

Creating Your Personal Inflammatory Profile

As you complete your systematic elimination and reintroduction process, compile your findings into a comprehensive personal inflammatory profile.

Your Inflammatory Trigger List:

Document foods and exposures that consistently cause:

- Immediate reactions (within 2 hours)
- Delayed reactions (12-72 hours)
- Cumulative reactions (only problematic with repeated exposure)
- Dose-dependent reactions (problematic only in large quantities)

Your Anti-Inflammatory Superstars:

Identify foods and practices that consistently improve your symptoms:
- Foods that boost energy and improve mood
- Practices that enhance sleep quality
- Activities that reduce stress and improve resilience
- Supplements or herbs that provide consistent benefits

Your Tolerance Thresholds:

Many people can tolerate small amounts of their trigger foods occasionally:
- Frequency limits (how often you can consume trigger foods)
- Quantity limits (how much you can consume at once)
- Timing considerations (when trigger foods are best tolerated)
- Combination effects (foods that are problematic together but not alone)

Implementing Your Personalized Anti-Inflammatory Strategy

Your personal inflammatory fingerprint provides the roadmap for creating a sustainable, effective anti-inflammatory lifestyle. This individualized approach is far more powerful than following generic dietary guidelines because it addresses your specific biological responses.

The 80/20 Principle:

Focus 80% of your efforts on the strategies that provide the greatest impact for your specific inflammatory pattern:
- Consistently avoid your major inflammatory triggers
- Regularly include your anti-inflammatory superstar foods

- Maintain the lifestyle practices that support your inflammatory resolution
- Address your genetic and gender-specific vulnerabilities

Reserve 20% of your flexibility for:
- Social situations and special occasions
- Experimenting with new foods and approaches
- Adapting to changing life circumstances
- Managing stress-related dietary choices

Your inflammatory fingerprint will evolve as you age, experience life changes, and optimize your health. Plan to reassess your triggers and responses annually, or whenever you experience significant life changes, health challenges, or improvements in your inflammatory status.

The investment in understanding your unique inflammatory fingerprint pays dividends throughout your lifetime. By working with your individual biology rather than against it, you can achieve lasting improvements in energy, mood, physical symptoms, and overall quality of life while avoiding the frustration of one-size-fits-all approaches that ignore your personal needs.

Chapter 2

The Gut-Brain-Inflammation Axis

Your gut and brain are in constant communication through a sophisticated network that directly controls your inflammatory response. This connection, known as the gut-brain-inflammation axis, represents one of the most powerful leverage points for reducing chronic inflammation throughout your body. Understanding and optimizing this system can provide dramatic improvements in both physical and mental symptoms that may have puzzled you for years.

The relationship between your digestive system, nervous system, and immune system is so intimate that dysfunction in one area inevitably affects the others. When your gut becomes inflamed and permeable, it triggers brain inflammation that affects mood, cognition, and stress responses. When your brain perceives chronic stress, it disrupts gut function and promotes intestinal inflammation. This creates self-perpetuating cycles that can trap you in chronic inflammatory states.

The encouraging news is that this interconnected system also means that healing interventions applied to one area can create positive cascading effects throughout the entire network. By strategically addressing gut health, nervous system function, stress responses, and circadian rhythms simultaneously, you can break inflammatory cycles and restore healthy communication between these critical systems.

How Intestinal Permeability Drives Systemic Inflammation

Your intestinal wall represents the largest interface between your internal body and the external environment. This barrier, consisting of a single layer of cells held together by tight junction proteins, must perform the seemingly impossible task of allowing beneficial nutrients to enter your bloodstream while keeping harmful substances out.

When functioning properly, your intestinal barrier maintains selective permeability, welcoming nutrients while excluding toxins, partially digested food particles, and pathogenic microorganisms. However, multiple factors in modern life can compromise this barrier, creating a condition commonly known as "leaky gut" or increased intestinal permeability.

The Architecture of Intestinal Barrier Function

Your intestinal barrier consists of multiple layers of protection working together to maintain selective permeability. The outermost layer contains beneficial bacteria that compete with harmful microorganisms for space and nutrients. Beneath this lies a protective mucus layer that traps pathogens and provides a medium for beneficial bacteria to thrive.

The actual cellular barrier consists of intestinal epithelial cells connected by tight junction proteins that act like adjustable gates. These junctions can open and close in response to various signals, allowing nutrients to pass through while maintaining protection against harmful substances.

Supporting this physical barrier is your gut-associated lymphoid tissue (GALT), which contains approximately 70% of your immune system. This immune surveillance system constantly monitors the contents of your digestive tract, ready to mount inflammatory responses against genuine threats while maintaining tolerance to food and beneficial bacteria.

The Perfect Storm: How Modern Life Damages Your Intestinal Barrier

Multiple factors in contemporary life conspire to damage your intestinal barrier, creating the perfect conditions for increased permeability and systemic inflammation.

Dietary Damage to Intestinal Integrity

Processed foods contain numerous compounds that directly damage your intestinal barrier. Emulsifiers, commonly used in processed foods to improve texture and shelf life, strip away the protective mucus layer and allow bacteria to contact intestinal cells directly. This bacterial contact triggers inflammatory responses that weaken tight junctions.

Refined sugars feed harmful bacteria and yeast in your digestive tract, allowing them to overgrow and produce inflammatory compounds. These microorganisms can directly damage intestinal cells and produce toxins that increase intestinal permeability.

Industrial seed oils, consumed in unprecedented quantities through processed foods, become incorporated into cell membranes throughout your digestive tract. These unstable oils make intestinal cells more susceptible to damage from oxidative stress and inflammatory compounds.

Gluten, a protein found in wheat, barley, and rye, triggers the release of zonulin, a protein that directly opens tight junctions in all people, not just those with celiac disease. While healthy individuals can typically handle occasional gluten exposure, chronic consumption can contribute to persistent intestinal permeability.

Pharmaceutical Assault on Gut Barrier Function

Several classes of commonly used medications can significantly damage your intestinal barrier. Nonsteroidal anti-inflammatory drugs (NSAIDs) like ibuprofen and naproxen directly damage intestinal cells and increase permeability within hours of consumption. Even occasional use can contribute to barrier dysfunction, while chronic use virtually guarantees increased intestinal permeability.

Antibiotics destroy beneficial bacteria that maintain barrier function while allowing harmful microorganisms to proliferate. A single course of antibiotics can disrupt your intestinal microbiome for months, reducing the protective bacterial layer and increasing susceptibility to intestinal damage.

Proton pump inhibitors, commonly prescribed for acid reflux, reduce stomach acid production to dangerously low levels. This allows harmful bacteria to survive passage through the stomach and colonize the small intestine, where they can damage the intestinal barrier and trigger inflammatory responses.

Stress-Induced Intestinal Damage

Chronic psychological stress directly damages your intestinal barrier through multiple mechanisms. Stress hormones like cortisol reduce the production of protective mucus and weaken tight junction proteins. Stress also redirects blood flow away from digestive organs, reducing their ability to maintain and repair the intestinal barrier.

The stress response activates your sympathetic nervous system, which suppresses digestive function and reduces the production of digestive enzymes and stomach acid. This creates an environment where food is incompletely digested, producing larger protein fragments that are more likely to trigger immune responses if they cross the intestinal barrier.

The Inflammatory Cascade: From Leaky Gut to Systemic Inflammation

When your intestinal barrier becomes compromised, partially digested food particles, bacterial components, and toxins gain access to your bloodstream. Your immune system recognizes these substances as foreign invaders and mounts inflammatory responses to neutralize them.

Molecular Mimicry and Autoimmune Reactions

Some of the protein fragments that escape through your compromised intestinal barrier bear structural similarities to proteins in your own tissues. This phenomenon, called molecular mimicry, can trigger your immune system to attack your own tissues, leading to autoimmune reactions.

For example, gliadin proteins from wheat can trigger immune responses against thyroid tissue, contributing to autoimmune thyroid conditions. Dairy proteins can mimic proteins in joint tissues, potentially contributing to rheumatoid arthritis in susceptible individuals.

Liver Overwhelm and Systemic Toxicity

Substances that escape through your intestinal barrier travel directly to your liver via the portal circulation. Your liver must process and detoxify these compounds, but chronic exposure can overwhelm your liver's detoxification capacity.

When your liver becomes overwhelmed, toxins and inflammatory compounds circulate throughout your body, triggering inflammatory responses in distant tissues. This explains why intestinal permeability can contribute to seemingly unrelated conditions like skin problems, joint pain, brain fog, and mood disorders.

Systemic Immune Activation

Chronic exposure to substances that shouldn't be in your bloodstream keeps your immune system in a state of persistent activation. This ongoing immune stimulation depletes immune resources, reduces your ability to fight genuine infections, and contributes to the development of chronic inflammatory conditions.

Healing Your Intestinal Barrier: The 4R Protocol

Repairing intestinal permeability requires a systematic approach that addresses the underlying causes while supporting your body's natural healing mechanisms. The 4R protocol—Remove, Replace, Reinoculate, and Repair—provides a comprehensive framework for restoring intestinal barrier function.

Remove: Eliminating Intestinal Irritants

The first step involves removing substances that damage your intestinal barrier:

➤ Dietary Removals:
- Eliminate processed foods containing emulsifiers, preservatives, and artificial additives
- Remove refined sugars and artificial sweeteners that feed harmful bacteria
- Avoid industrial seed oils and fried foods that damage intestinal cell membranes
- Consider removing gluten-containing grains, at least temporarily
- Identify and eliminate personal food sensitivities discovered through your elimination protocol

➤ Lifestyle Modifications:
- Minimize unnecessary antibiotic use and discuss alternatives with your healthcare provider
- Avoid NSAIDs when possible, using natural anti-inflammatory approaches instead
- Address underlying digestive issues that may require acid-blocking medications
- Implement stress management techniques to reduce stress-induced intestinal damage

Replace: Restoring Digestive Function

Support your body's natural digestive processes to ensure complete food breakdown:

➤ Digestive Support Strategies:
- Begin meals with bitter foods or herbs to stimulate digestive enzyme production
- Chew food thoroughly to begin the digestive process in your mouth
- Eat in a relaxed environment to activate your parasympathetic nervous system
- Consider digestive enzyme supplements with meals if you experience digestive symptoms
- Support stomach acid production with apple cider vinegar or lemon juice before meals

➤ Nutrient Replacement:
- Address nutrient deficiencies that impair intestinal barrier function
- Focus on nutrients critical for barrier integrity: zinc, vitamin A, vitamin D, and omega-3 fatty acids
- Include foods rich in glutamine, the primary fuel for intestinal cells
- Consume adequate protein to support tissue repair and immune function

Reinoculate: Restoring Beneficial Bacteria

Rebuild your beneficial bacterial populations to restore protective barrier function:

➢ Probiotic Foods:
- Include fermented vegetables like sauerkraut, kimchi, and fermented pickles
- Consume fermented dairy products like kefir and yogurt if you tolerate dairy
- Try fermented beverages like kombucha and water kefir
- Include miso, tempeh, and other fermented soy products if appropriate

➢ Prebiotic Support:
- Consume foods that feed beneficial bacteria: Jerusalem artichokes, onions, garlic, leeks
- Include resistant starch sources like cooled potatoes and green bananas
- Add inulin-rich foods like chicory root and dandelion greens
- Include polyphenol-rich foods that support beneficial bacterial growth

➢ Targeted Probiotic Supplementation:
Consider specific probiotic strains that have been shown to support intestinal barrier function:
- Lactobacillus plantarum for reducing intestinal permeability
- Bifidobacterium infantis for supporting immune regulation
- Saccharomyces boulardii for protecting against antibiotic-associated damage
- Multi-strain formulas that include barrier-protective species

Repair: Supporting Intestinal Healing

Provide your intestinal cells with the nutrients they need for repair and regeneration:

➢ Barrier-Healing Nutrients:
- L-glutamine: The primary fuel for intestinal cells and a key component of tight junction proteins
- Zinc: Essential for protein synthesis and wound healing throughout the digestive tract
- Vitamin A: Critical for maintaining healthy mucus production and immune function
- Omega-3 fatty acids: Reduce inflammation and support healthy cell membrane function

- Collagen peptides: Provide building blocks for intestinal tissue repair

➢ Healing Foods and Preparations:
- Bone broth rich in collagen, gelatin, and healing amino acids
- Slippery elm tea to soothe and protect intestinal tissues
- Marshmallow root preparations that coat and heal inflamed tissues
- Aloe vera juice (inner leaf only) for its anti-inflammatory and healing properties
- Fermented cod liver oil for vitamins A and D plus omega-3 fatty acids

The Vagus Nerve's Role in Inflammatory Control

Your vagus nerve represents the primary communication highway between your brain and your digestive system, playing a crucial role in controlling inflammation throughout your body. This remarkable nerve, the longest in your autonomic nervous system, carries signals that can either promote or suppress inflammatory responses depending on its level of activation and health.

Understanding and optimizing vagus nerve function provides one of the most powerful tools for reducing chronic inflammation while improving stress resilience, digestive health, and overall wellbeing. The vagus nerve's anti-inflammatory effects are so significant that researchers have developed vagus nerve stimulation devices as medical treatments for inflammatory conditions.

The Vagus Nerve: Your Body's Anti-Inflammatory Superhighway

Your vagus nerve originates in your brainstem and travels throughout your body, connecting your brain to your heart, lungs, digestive organs, and immune system. This extensive network allows your brain to monitor and control inflammatory responses in real-time based on your body's needs and environmental circumstances.

The vagus nerve consists of approximately 80% sensory fibers that carry information from your body to your brain, and 20% motor fibers that carry commands from your brain to your organs. This bidirectional communication allows for sophisticated control of inflammatory responses based on both internal body conditions and external environmental factors.

The Inflammatory Reflex: Your Body's Built-In Anti-Inflammatory System

One of the vagus nerve's most important functions is mediating the inflammatory reflex, also known as the cholinergic anti-inflammatory pathway. When your brain detects inflammation in your body through vagus nerve sensory fibers, it can respond by sending anti-inflammatory signals back through the motor fibers.

These anti-inflammatory signals trigger the release of acetylcholine, a neurotransmitter that binds to receptors on immune cells and directly suppresses the production of inflammatory cytokines. This system allows your brain to fine-tune inflammatory responses, ensuring that inflammation remains appropriate to the threat and resolves when no longer needed.

The inflammatory reflex represents evolution's solution to preventing excessive inflammatory responses that could damage healthy tissues. However, this system requires optimal vagus nerve function to work effectively, and many aspects of modern life can impair vagal function and disrupt this critical anti-inflammatory mechanism.

Signs of Vagus Nerve Dysfunction

Poor vagus nerve function, also called low vagal tone, contributes to chronic inflammation and a wide range of health problems. Recognizing the signs of vagal dysfunction can help you identify whether optimizing your vagus nerve function should be a priority in your anti-inflammatory strategy.

➢ Physical Signs of Low Vagal Tone:
- Chronic digestive problems including bloating, constipation, or gastroparesis
- Difficulty swallowing or frequent choking on food or drinks
- Chronic inflammation and slow healing from injuries or infections
- Heart rate variability problems and poor stress recovery
- Chronic fatigue and poor exercise recovery
- Frequent infections and compromised immune function
- Blood pressure regulation problems
- Temperature regulation difficulties

➢ Mental and Emotional Signs:
- Difficulty managing stress and poor stress resilience
- Anxiety, particularly social anxiety and panic attacks
- Depression and mood instability
- Difficulty with emotional regulation and mood swings
- Problems with focus, concentration, and cognitive function
- Insomnia and poor sleep quality
- Reduced motivation and sense of wellbeing

➢ Digestive and Metabolic Signs:
- Gastroparesis (delayed stomach emptying)
- Gastroesophageal reflux disease (GERD)
- Irritable bowel syndrome (IBS) symptoms
- Small intestinal bacterial overgrowth (SIBO)
- Food sensitivities and digestive intolerance
- Blood sugar regulation problems
- Difficulty losing weight despite appropriate diet and exercise

Optimizing Vagus Nerve Function: Natural Vagal Toning Strategies

Fortunately, you can improve vagus nerve function through targeted lifestyle interventions that stimulate and strengthen vagal pathways. These practices, collectively known as vagal toning, can significantly enhance your body's natural anti-inflammatory responses.

Breathing Techniques for Vagal Stimulation

Deep, slow breathing represents one of the most accessible and effective methods for stimulating your vagus nerve. Specific breathing patterns can activate the parasympathetic nervous system and strengthen vagal tone over time.

➢ 4-7-8 Breathing Protocol:
- Inhale through your nose for 4 counts
- Hold your breath for 7 counts
- Exhale through your mouth for 8 counts
- Repeat 4-8 cycles, practicing 2-3 times daily

➢ Box Breathing for Stress Recovery:
- Inhale for 4 counts
- Hold for 4 counts
- Exhale for 4 counts
- Hold empty for 4 counts
- Continue for 5-10 minutes during stressful situations

➢ Humming and Singing:
The vibrations created by humming, singing, or chanting stimulate your vagus nerve through its connections to your throat and vocal cords. Regular practice can improve vagal tone while providing immediate stress relief.

Cold Exposure for Vagal Strengthening

Controlled cold exposure activates your vagus nerve and strengthens your stress response systems. Start gradually and build tolerance over time:

➢ Cold Shower Protocol:
- Begin with 30 seconds of cold water at the end of your regular shower
- Gradually increase duration to 2-3 minutes over several weeks
- Focus on deep, controlled breathing during cold exposure
- Practice 3-5 times per week for optimal benefits

➢ Cold Water Swimming or Ice Baths:
For more advanced practitioners, cold water swimming or ice baths provide more intense vagal stimulation. Always practice safely and consider medical consultation if you have cardiovascular conditions.

Movement and Exercise for Vagal Health

Specific types of physical activity can enhance vagus nerve function while providing general health benefits:

➢ Yoga and Gentle Movement:

- Focus on poses that compress the abdomen and stimulate digestion
- Include inversions that activate the parasympathetic nervous system
- Practice slow, mindful movements coordinated with breath
- Emphasize relaxation and stress reduction over intense physical challenge

➢ Walking and Nature Exposure:
- Regular walking, particularly in natural environments, supports vagal tone
- Focus on rhythmic, comfortable paces that allow for easy breathing
- Include mindful attention to your surroundings and sensory experiences
- Aim for 30-45 minutes of walking daily when possible

Digestive Practices for Vagal Optimization

Since your vagus nerve extensively innervates your digestive system, digestive practices can significantly impact vagal function:

➢ Mindful Eating Practices:
- Eat in a calm, relaxed environment free from distractions
- Chew food thoroughly and eat slowly to activate digestive reflexes
- Practice gratitude or mindfulness before meals to activate parasympathetic responses
- Avoid eating when stressed or emotionally upset

➢ Intermittent Fasting:
Strategic fasting periods can enhance vagal tone and improve metabolic flexibility:
- Start with 12-hour overnight fasts
- Gradually extend to 14-16 hour fasting windows if appropriate
- Focus on nutrient-dense foods during eating windows
- Monitor energy levels and adjust fasting duration accordingly

Advanced Vagal Optimization Techniques

For individuals with significant vagal dysfunction or those seeking to optimize performance, more advanced techniques can provide additional benefits:

Heart Rate Variability Training

Heart rate variability (HRV) represents a direct measure of vagus nerve function. HRV training involves using biofeedback devices to learn to control your heart rate patterns through breathing and relaxation techniques.

➤ HRV Training Protocol:
- Use a validated HRV device or smartphone app
- Practice coherent breathing (5-6 breaths per minute) while monitoring HRV
- Aim for 10-20 minutes of daily practice
- Track progress over time and adjust techniques based on results

Gargling and Vocal Exercises

The vagus nerve connects to muscles in your throat and soft palate. Exercises that engage these muscles can stimulate vagal function:

➤ Daily Gargling Practice:
- Gargle with water for 30-60 seconds, 2-3 times daily
- Use warm salt water for additional antimicrobial benefits
- Focus on creating strong vibrations in your throat
- Practice consistently for several weeks to see benefits

➤ Vocal Toning Exercises:
- Practice humming, chanting, or toning sounds like "Om" or "Ahh"
- Focus on feeling vibrations in your chest and throat
- Include singing as a regular practice if enjoyable
- Join a choir or singing group for social and vagal benefits

Stress-Inflammation Feedback Loops and Breaking the Cycle

The relationship between stress and inflammation creates powerful feedback loops that can trap you in cycles of chronic activation.

Understanding these loops and implementing targeted interventions to break them represents a crucial component of any comprehensive anti-inflammatory strategy.

Stress and inflammation feed each other in ways that can create self-perpetuating cycles. Chronic stress triggers inflammatory responses that damage tissues and impair function. This damage creates physical stress on your body, which triggers more stress hormones and inflammatory responses. Meanwhile, inflammation directly affects brain function, making you more sensitive to stress and less able to cope with challenges effectively.

The Physiology of Stress-Induced Inflammation

When you perceive stress, your brain activates your hypothalamic-pituitary-adrenal (HPA) axis, triggering the release of stress hormones like cortisol and adrenaline. These hormones prepare your body for immediate action by mobilizing energy, increasing heart rate, and temporarily suppressing non-essential functions like digestion and immune responses.

In acute situations, this stress response is protective and appropriate. However, chronic stress keeps these systems activated continuously, leading to dysregulation and inflammatory consequences.

Cortisol Dysregulation and Inflammatory Consequences

Cortisol normally helps regulate inflammation by suppressing excessive immune responses. However, chronic stress can lead to two problematic patterns: persistently elevated cortisol or cortisol resistance, where tissues become less responsive to cortisol's anti-inflammatory effects.

Persistently elevated cortisol suppresses beneficial immune functions while promoting inflammatory responses in certain tissues. It increases blood sugar, promotes fat storage around your midsection, disrupts sleep patterns, and impairs digestive function.

Cortisol resistance develops when tissues become less responsive to cortisol's signals due to chronic exposure. This allows inflammatory responses to proceed unchecked while maintaining the negative effects of elevated cortisol production.

Stress-Induced Gut Dysfunction

Chronic stress significantly impairs digestive function through multiple mechanisms. Stress hormones reduce stomach acid production, slow digestive motility, and impair the production of digestive enzymes. This creates conditions for bacterial overgrowth, increased intestinal permeability, and food sensitivities.

The gut-brain connection means that digestive dysfunction directly affects your brain's stress response systems. An inflamed, dysfunctional digestive system sends signals to your brain that increase anxiety, depression, and stress sensitivity, creating a vicious cycle of stress and digestive problems.

Neuroinflammation and Stress Sensitivity

Chronic stress promotes inflammation in brain tissues, particularly in areas responsible for mood regulation, memory, and stress response. This neuroinflammation makes you more sensitive to stress, reduces your resilience, and impairs your ability to cope with challenges effectively.

Neuroinflammation also disrupts neurotransmitter production and signaling, contributing to anxiety, depression, and cognitive problems. These mental health challenges create additional stress, perpetuating the inflammatory cycle.

Breaking the Stress-Inflammation Cycle: Integrated Interventions

Successfully breaking stress-inflammation cycles requires interventions that address both the stress response and inflammatory processes simultaneously. This integrated approach provides synergistic benefits that are greater than addressing either component alone.

Stress Response Retraining

Learning to manage your stress response more effectively reduces the inflammatory burden of chronic stress activation:

➢ Cognitive Reframing Techniques:
- Identify catastrophic thinking patterns that amplify stress responses
- Practice realistic assessment of threats and challenges
- Develop problem-solving strategies for controllable stressors
- Learn to accept and adapt to uncontrollable circumstances

➢ Mindfulness and Meditation Practices:
- Regular meditation practice reduces baseline stress hormone levels
- Mindfulness techniques help you respond rather than react to stressors
- Body awareness practices help you recognize stress signals early
- Loving-kindness meditation reduces inflammatory markers while improving mood

➢ Progressive Muscle Relaxation:
- Systematic tensing and releasing of muscle groups activates relaxation responses
- Regular practice improves your ability to release physical tension
- Combines well with breathing exercises for enhanced benefits
- Can be practiced anywhere and requires no special equipment

Anti-Inflammatory Stress Management

Certain stress management techniques provide both stress reduction and direct anti-inflammatory benefits:

➢ Forest Bathing and Nature Immersion:
- Time spent in natural environments reduces cortisol and inflammatory markers
- Phytoncides (compounds released by trees) have direct anti-inflammatory effects
- Natural settings promote relaxation and stress recovery
- Regular nature exposure improves immune function and resilience

➢ Social Connection and Community:
- Strong social relationships reduce inflammatory markers and stress hormones
- Social support buffers the inflammatory effects of stress
- Community activities provide purpose and meaning that enhance resilience
- Isolation and loneliness are significant inflammatory stressors

➢ Creative Expression and Play:
- Creative activities activate brain regions associated with relaxation and flow states
- Artistic expression provides emotional outlets that reduce stress accumulation
- Play and humor have direct anti-inflammatory effects
- Creative pursuits provide meaning and purpose that enhance stress resilience

Nutritional Support for Stress-Inflammation Cycles

Specific nutrients can help break stress-inflammation cycles by supporting healthy stress responses while reducing inflammatory burden:

Adaptogenic Herbs for Stress Resilience

Adaptogenic herbs help your body adapt to stress more effectively while providing anti-inflammatory benefits:

➢ Ashwagandha:
- Reduces cortisol levels and improves stress resilience
- Provides anti-inflammatory and antioxidant benefits
- Supports healthy sleep patterns and energy levels
- Take 300-600mg daily, preferably with meals

➢ Rhodiola Rosea:
- Enhances mental performance under stress
- Reduces fatigue and improves mood
- Provides antioxidant and anti-inflammatory effects
- Take 200-400mg daily, preferably in the morning

➢ Holy Basil (Tulsi):
- Supports healthy cortisol rhythms
- Provides adaptogenic and anti-inflammatory benefits
- Can be consumed as tea throughout the day
- Particularly beneficial for stress-related digestive issues

Nutrients for Stress Response Support

Key nutrients that support healthy stress responses and reduce inflammation:

➢ Magnesium:
- Essential for nervous system function and stress response regulation
- Deficiency is common and contributes to stress sensitivity
- Anti-inflammatory and muscle-relaxing properties
- Include magnesium-rich foods like leafy greens, nuts, and seeds

➢ B-Complex Vitamins:
- Required for neurotransmitter production and stress hormone metabolism
- Depleted rapidly during periods of high stress
- Support energy production and nervous system function
- Focus on whole food sources like nutritional yeast and organ meats

➢ Omega-3 Fatty Acids:
- Directly reduce inflammatory responses to stress
- Support brain health and neurotransmitter function
- Improve mood and reduce anxiety
- Emphasize EPA-rich fish oil or marine sources

Circadian Rhythm Disruption as an Inflammatory Trigger

Your circadian rhythms orchestrate the timing of virtually every biological process in your body, including inflammatory responses. When these rhythms become disrupted, the carefully coordinated anti-inflammatory processes that normally occur during sleep and rest periods become dysregulated, leading to chronic inflammatory activation.

Modern life presents unprecedented challenges to maintaining healthy circadian rhythms. Artificial light exposure, irregular sleep schedules, shift work, frequent travel across time zones, and constant screen time all contribute to circadian disruption that promotes inflammation throughout your body.

Your body's inflammatory responses follow predictable daily patterns controlled by your internal biological clock. Understanding these patterns helps you optimize your daily routine to support natural anti-inflammatory processes.

The Daily Inflammatory Rhythm

Under normal circumstances, inflammatory markers like cortisol and various cytokines follow specific daily patterns:

➢ Morning (6 AM - 12 PM):
- Cortisol levels peak in the early morning to help you wake up and handle daily stressors
- Pro-inflammatory cytokines are naturally higher to support alertness and immune surveillance
- This inflammatory activation is normal and necessary for optimal daytime function

➢ Afternoon (12 PM - 6 PM):
- Inflammatory markers gradually decline as cortisol levels decrease
- Your body begins shifting toward repair and recovery processes
- This transition period is crucial for maintaining inflammatory balance

➢ Evening (6 PM - 10 PM):
- Anti-inflammatory processes become more active as melatonin production begins
- Your body prepares for the restorative processes that occur during sleep
- Light exposure during this period can disrupt these anti-inflammatory preparations

➢ Night (10 PM - 6 AM):
- Peak anti-inflammatory activity occurs during deep sleep phases
- Growth hormone release supports tissue repair and immune system regeneration

- Your brain's glymphatic system clears inflammatory waste products
- Disruption of sleep during this period has the most severe inflammatory consequences

Circadian Immune System Regulation

Your immune system function varies dramatically throughout the day, with different types of immune responses being more active at different times. This variation helps optimize your body's ability to fight infections when you're most likely to encounter them while promoting healing and recovery during rest periods.

Disruption of these natural rhythms can leave you more susceptible to infections, slower to heal from injuries, and more prone to autoimmune reactions where your immune system attacks your own tissues.

Multiple aspects of contemporary life work together to disrupt your natural circadian rhythms and promote chronic inflammation:

Artificial Light Exposure

Electric lighting, particularly blue light from screens and LED bulbs, represents one of the most significant circadian disruptors in modern life. Your brain interprets light exposure as a signal that it's daytime, suppressing melatonin production and maintaining inflammatory activation even when you should be transitioning to anti-inflammatory nighttime processes.

➢ Sources of Problematic Light Exposure:
- Smartphones, tablets, and computer screens used in the evening
- LED light bulbs and fluorescent lighting in homes and workplaces
- Street lights and other outdoor lighting that enters bedrooms
- Television viewing, particularly in darkened rooms
- Early morning artificial light exposure before natural sunrise

Irregular Sleep and Meal Timing

Your circadian rhythms depend on consistent timing signals to maintain proper coordination. Irregular sleep schedules, frequent time zone changes, and erratic meal timing all disrupt these signals and promote inflammatory dysregulation.

> Timing Disruptions That Promote Inflammation:

- Varying bedtimes and wake times, even on weekends
- Eating large meals late in the evening when digestion should be winding down
- Skipping breakfast, which provides important circadian timing signals
- Frequent travel across multiple time zones
- Shift work that requires alertness during natural sleep hours

Stress and Circadian Disruption

Chronic stress disrupts circadian rhythms by keeping cortisol levels elevated at inappropriate times. This prevents the natural decline in cortisol that should occur in the evening and disrupts the coordination between your stress response system and your circadian clock.

Restoring Circadian Rhythm for Anti-Inflammatory Benefits

Optimizing your circadian rhythms provides powerful anti-inflammatory benefits while improving sleep quality, energy levels, and overall health. The key is to provide consistent, appropriate timing signals that help your internal clock maintain proper coordination.

Light Exposure Optimization

Strategic light exposure represents the most powerful tool for optimizing circadian rhythms:

> Morning Light Protocol:
- Get bright light exposure within 30 minutes of waking, preferably from natural sunlight
- Spend 10-30 minutes outdoors or near a bright window
- Use a 10,000 lux light therapy device if natural light is insufficient

- Avoid wearing sunglasses during morning light exposure unless medically necessary

> Daytime Light Strategies:
- Maximize natural light exposure throughout the day
- Take regular breaks outdoors, especially during midday
- Position work areas near windows when possible
- Use bright, full-spectrum lighting in indoor environments

> Evening Light Management:
- Dim lights 2-3 hours before bedtime
- Use warm, amber-colored lights in the evening
- Install blue light blocking software on electronic devices
- Consider blue light blocking glasses for evening screen use
- Create a completely dark sleeping environment

Meal Timing for Circadian Health

When you eat has profound effects on your circadian rhythms and inflammatory patterns:

> Circadian Meal Timing Strategies:
- Eat your largest meal earlier in the day when digestive function is optimal
- Stop eating 3-4 hours before bedtime to allow digestion to complete
- Maintain consistent meal timing even on weekends
- Consider time-restricted eating windows that align with natural circadian patterns
- Include protein in your breakfast to provide strong circadian timing signals

> Foods That Support Circadian Function:
- Tart cherry juice in the evening provides natural melatonin
- Magnesium-rich foods support relaxation and sleep quality
- Complex carbohydrates in the evening can support serotonin production
- Avoid caffeine after 2 PM to prevent sleep disruption

Sleep Optimization for Anti-Inflammatory Benefits

Quality sleep represents your body's primary opportunity for anti-inflammatory recovery and repair:

➤ Sleep Environment Optimization:
- Maintain bedroom temperature between 65-68°F (18-20°C)
- Use blackout curtains or eye masks to eliminate light exposure
- Minimize noise with earplugs or white noise machines
- Choose comfortable, supportive bedding materials
- Remove electronic devices from the bedroom

➤ Sleep Hygiene Practices:
- Maintain consistent bedtime and wake time schedules
- Develop a relaxing bedtime routine that begins 1-2 hours before sleep
- Avoid stimulating activities like intense exercise or work before bed
- Practice relaxation techniques like progressive muscle relaxation or meditation
- Keep a sleep diary to identify patterns and areas for improvement

Managing Shift Work and Travel

For individuals who must work irregular schedules or travel frequently, specific strategies can minimize circadian disruption:

➤ Shift Work Strategies:
- Use bright light exposure during work hours to maintain alertness
- Wear sunglasses on the drive home to prevent morning light exposure
- Create a dark, quiet sleep environment for daytime sleep
- Consider melatonin supplementation to support sleep timing
- Maintain consistent meal timing based on your work schedule

➤ Travel and Jet Lag Management:
- Begin adjusting sleep schedule 3-4 days before travel
- Use strategic light exposure to shift circadian rhythms
- Consider melatonin supplementation for eastward travel
- Stay hydrated and avoid alcohol during travel
- Immediately adopt local meal and sleep timing upon arrival

Chapter 3

Beyond Omega-3s: The Complete Anti-Inflammatory Nutrient Matrix

Most people who understand the basics of anti-inflammatory nutrition focus primarily on omega-3 fatty acids. While these essential fats are indeed crucial for managing inflammation, they represent just one piece of a much larger nutritional puzzle. Your body's inflammatory response system depends on a complex network of nutrients working together in precise ratios and combinations.

Understanding this complete anti-inflammatory nutrient matrix allows you to move beyond basic supplementation and create powerful synergistic effects through strategic food choices and nutrient combinations. This comprehensive approach can provide far more dramatic results than simply taking fish oil and hoping for the best.

The Polyphenol Orchestra: How Plant Compounds Create Anti-Inflammatory Symphony

Polyphenols represent one of nature's most sophisticated anti-inflammatory systems. These plant compounds don't work in isolation—they function like an orchestra, with each compound playing a specific role while harmonizing with others to create effects far greater than the sum of their parts.

Your body has evolved intricate systems for recognizing, absorbing, and utilizing these plant compounds, but only when they're consumed in the complex combinations found in whole foods. This is why isolated polyphenol supplements often fail to provide the benefits seen with polyphenol-rich foods.

The Four Classes of Anti-Inflammatory Polyphenols

➢ Flavonoids: The Inflammation Modulators

Flavonoids represent the largest and most diverse class of polyphenols, with over 6,000 different compounds identified. Each subclass provides specific anti-inflammatory benefits:

- Anthocyanins give berries their deep red, purple, and blue colors while providing powerful anti-inflammatory effects. These compounds specifically target the inflammatory pathways involved in cardiovascular disease and neuroinflammation. You'll find the highest concentrations in elderberries, black currants, blueberries, and purple cabbage.

- Quercetin acts as a natural antihistamine and mast cell stabilizer, making it particularly valuable for people with allergic inflammation. This flavonoid is abundant in onions, capers, lovage, and dill, but requires specific combinations with other compounds for optimal absorption.

- Catechins, found primarily in green tea, provide neuroprotective benefits and support healthy inflammatory resolution in brain tissues. The most potent catechin, EGCG, works synergistically with vitamin C and requires specific brewing techniques to maximize bioavailability.

- Hesperidin and other citrus flavonoids support vascular health and reduce inflammatory damage to blood vessels. These compounds work best when consumed with the whole fruit, including the white pith that contains complementary compounds.

➢ Phenolic Acids: The Cellular Protectors

Phenolic acids provide direct antioxidant protection to your cell membranes while supporting your body's natural antioxidant enzyme systems. Unlike flavonoids, phenolic acids are more easily absorbed and provide rapid anti-inflammatory effects.

- Chlorogenic acid, abundant in coffee and certain fruits, specifically targets metabolic inflammation and helps regulate blood sugar responses. However, the roasting process significantly affects chlorogenic acid content, making brewing method and bean selection crucial factors.
- Ferulic acid protects your skin and other tissues from inflammatory damage while supporting collagen production. You'll find high concentrations in whole grains, but only if they're prepared properly to break down the fiber matrix that binds these compounds.
- Ellagic acid provides particularly powerful anti-inflammatory effects in your digestive system and may help prevent inflammatory damage that leads to cellular dysfunction. Pomegranates, walnuts, and berries provide the highest concentrations, but absorption requires specific preparation methods.

➢ Stilbenes: The Longevity Compounds

Stilbenes like resveratrol have gained attention for their potential longevity benefits, but their primary mechanism involves modulating inflammatory pathways and supporting cellular repair processes.

- Resveratrol activates cellular pathways that enhance inflammatory resolution and protect against age-related inflammatory damage. While red wine contains resveratrol, you can obtain higher concentrations from purple grape skins, Japanese knotweed, and certain berries.
- Pterostilbene, found in blueberries and grapes, provides similar benefits to resveratrol but with better bioavailability and longer-lasting effects in your body.

➢ Lignans: The Hormone Balancers

Lignans provide anti-inflammatory benefits while helping to balance hormone levels, making them particularly valuable for reducing hormone-related inflammation.

- Secoisolariciresinol from flax seeds supports healthy estrogen metabolism while providing direct anti-inflammatory effects. However,

whole flax seeds must be ground fresh to maximize lignan availability.
- Pinoresinol and *lariciresinol* from sesame seeds work synergistically with sesame's healthy fats to provide sustained anti-inflammatory benefits.

Creating Polyphenol Synergy Through Strategic Combinations

The key to maximizing polyphenol anti-inflammatory effects lies in consuming them in specific combinations that enhance absorption and biological activity.

The Absorption Enhancement Matrix

Many polyphenols have poor bioavailability when consumed alone but become highly effective when combined with specific enhancer compounds:

➢ Fat-Soluble Polyphenol Optimization:
- Consume carotenoids (from orange and red vegetables) with healthy fats
- Combine turmeric with black pepper and coconut oil or ghee
- Include olive oil with tomato-based dishes to enhance lycopene absorption
- Pair dark leafy greens with avocado or nuts for carotenoid uptake

➢ Water-Soluble Polyphenol Enhancement:
- Consume vitamin C-rich foods with iron-rich plants to enhance both nutrients
- Combine green tea with citrus to improve catechin absorption
- Include onions or garlic with other vegetables to enhance quercetin uptake
- Consume berries with a small amount of healthy fat for optimal anthocyanin absorption

The Timing Strategy for Maximum Impact

The timing of polyphenol consumption significantly affects their anti-inflammatory impact:

➢ Morning Polyphenol Loading:
Start your day with a diverse array of polyphenols to support your body's natural

detoxification processes and prepare your inflammatory response systems for daily challenges:
- Green tea with fresh lemon and a pinch of black pepper
- Mixed berry smoothie with spinach and ground flax seeds
- Colorful vegetable omelet with herbs and spices

➢ Meal-Specific Polyphenol Strategies:
- Include bitter compounds (like radicchio or endive) before meals to stimulate digestive function
- Consume anti-inflammatory spices with protein-rich meals to prevent postprandial inflammation
- End meals with polyphenol-rich teas or small amounts of dark chocolate

➢ Evening Anti-Inflammatory Support:
Choose polyphenols that support inflammatory resolution and prepare your body for restorative sleep:
- Tart cherry juice for natural melatonin and anthocyanins
- Chamomile tea for calming polyphenols
- A small serving of walnuts for omega-3s and ellagic acid

Building Your Personal Polyphenol Profile

Different people respond better to different polyphenol combinations based on their genetic makeup, current health status, and specific inflammatory challenges.

➢ For Cardiovascular Inflammation:
Focus on anthocyanins, resveratrol, and quercetin:
- Daily servings of deeply colored berries
- Regular consumption of red onions and garlic
- Moderate amounts of red wine or purple grape juice
- Dark chocolate with at least 70% cacao content

➢ For Neuroinflammation:
Emphasize compounds that cross the blood-brain barrier:
- Green tea catechins consumed between meals
- Turmeric with black pepper and healthy fats
- Blueberries and other anthocyanin-rich fruits
- Walnuts for combined omega-3s and polyphenols

➢ For Digestive Inflammation:
Choose polyphenols that support gut health:
- Green tea consumed away from meals
- Pomegranate for ellagic acid
- Fresh herbs like oregano, thyme, and rosemary
- Fermented foods that provide both polyphenols and probiotics

Sulfur Compounds: The Master Detoxifiers and Inflammation Resolvers

Sulfur compounds represent some of the most powerful anti-inflammatory nutrients available, yet they're often overlooked in standard nutritional approaches. These compounds support your body's natural detoxification systems while directly modulating inflammatory pathways.

The Cruciferous Connection: Glucosinolates and Isothiocyanates

Cruciferous vegetables like broccoli, cauliflower, cabbage, and kale contain glucosinolates that convert to isothiocyanates when you chew or chop these vegetables. This conversion process is crucial—glucosinolates themselves have minimal biological activity, but their isothiocyanate metabolites provide profound anti-inflammatory benefits.

➢ Sulforaphane: The Inflammation Resolution Activator

Sulforaphane, derived from glucoraphanin in broccoli and broccoli sprouts, represents one of the most potent naturally occurring anti-inflammatory compounds. This isothiocyanate activates your body's Nrf2 pathway, which controls the production of antioxidant enzymes and inflammatory resolution factors.

• Maximizing Sulforaphane Production:
- Choose broccoli sprouts over mature broccoli (up to 100 times higher glucoraphanin content)
- Chop or chew cruciferous vegetables thoroughly to activate myrosinase enzyme
- Allow chopped vegetables to sit for 10-15 minutes before cooking to maximize conversion

- Consume raw or lightly steamed—excessive heat destroys both myrosinase and sulforaphane
- Combine with mustard seed powder if cooking destroys natural myrosinase

➢ Indole-3-Carbinol: The Hormone Modulator

Indole-3-carbinol (I3C) and its metabolite diindolylmethane (DIM) support healthy hormone metabolism while reducing hormone-related inflammation. These compounds are particularly beneficial for reducing estrogen-driven inflammatory conditions.

• Optimizing I3C and DIM Benefits:
- Include a variety of cruciferous vegetables rather than focusing on one type
- Consume both raw and cooked cruciferous vegetables for different compound profiles
- Combine with healthy fats to enhance absorption
- Include probiotic foods to support beneficial gut bacteria that help metabolize these compounds

➢ Allium Compounds: The Immune System Modulators

Garlic, onions, leeks, and other allium vegetables contain sulfur compounds that provide powerful anti-inflammatory and immune-modulating effects.

➢ Allicin: The Antimicrobial Anti-Inflammatory

Allicin, formed when garlic is crushed or chopped, provides broad-spectrum antimicrobial effects while modulating inflammatory responses. This compound helps reduce inflammatory burden by addressing underlying infections that may be driving chronic inflammation.

• Maximizing Allicin Benefits:
- Crush or mince fresh garlic and allow it to sit for 10 minutes before using
- Consume garlic raw or add it to dishes at the end of cooking
- Combine with healthy fats to enhance absorption and reduce potential digestive irritation
- Include both garlic and onions for synergistic sulfur compound effects

➢ Quercetin and Sulfur Synergy

Onions provide a unique combination of quercetin and sulfur compounds that work synergistically to provide enhanced anti-inflammatory effects. The sulfur compounds in onions help stabilize quercetin and improve its bioavailability.

Sulfur-Containing Amino Acids: The Building Blocks of Detoxification

Your body requires adequate sulfur-containing amino acids to produce glutathione, your most important endogenous antioxidant and detoxification compound.

Cysteine and N-Acetylcysteine

Cysteine serves as the rate-limiting amino acid for glutathione production. While your body can produce some cysteine, inflammatory conditions often increase your requirements beyond what you can synthesize.

➢ Food Sources of Cysteine:
- High-quality animal proteins: poultry, fish, eggs
- Sunflower seeds and sesame seeds
- Oats and other whole grains
- Legumes, particularly lentils and chickpeas

Methionine and SAM-e Production

Methionine supports methylation reactions crucial for inflammatory resolution and neurotransmitter production. However, methionine requires adequate B-vitamins and must be balanced with glycine to prevent inflammatory metabolites.

➢ Optimizing Methionine Metabolism:
- Include B-vitamin rich foods with methionine-rich proteins
- Balance methionine intake with glycine from bone broth, gelatin, or collagen
- Support methylation with folate-rich leafy greens
- Include choline-rich foods like eggs and liver

Creating Your Sulfur Compound Strategy

➢ Daily Sulfur Compound Protocol:
- Include at least one serving of cruciferous vegetables daily
- Consume fresh garlic or onions with most meals
- Rotate between different sulfur-rich foods to maximize compound diversity
- Support sulfur metabolism with adequate B-vitamins and minerals

➢ Preparation Methods for Maximum Benefit:
- Raw preparations: sauerkraut, kimchi, fresh garlic, sprouts
- Minimal cooking: light steaming, quick sautéing, raw additions to cooked dishes
- Fermented options: fermented garlic, aged onions, cultured vegetables
- Strategic combinations: sulfur compounds with healthy fats and complementary nutrients

Critical Mineral Ratios: The Foundation of Anti-Inflammatory Balance

While individual minerals receive attention for their anti-inflammatory properties, the ratios between minerals often matter more than absolute amounts. Your body maintains delicate mineral balances that, when disrupted, can promote inflammatory responses even when individual mineral levels appear adequate.

The Zinc-Copper Seesaw: Balancing Immune Function and Antioxidant Activity

Zinc and copper work together in numerous enzymatic reactions crucial for inflammatory control. However, these minerals compete for absorption and cellular uptake, making their ratio more important than individual levels.

➢ The Optimal Zinc-Copper Ratio

Research suggests an optimal zinc-to-copper ratio between 8:1 and 12:1 for most people. However, modern diets often provide ratios as high as 50:1, creating copper deficiency that impairs antioxidant enzyme function and promotes inflammatory damage.

• Zinc's Anti-Inflammatory Roles:
- Supports immune system regulation and prevents excessive inflammatory responses
- Required for wound healing and tissue repair
- Necessary for proper insulin function and blood sugar control
- Supports healthy skin barrier function
- Required for neurotransmitter synthesis and mood regulation

• Signs of Zinc Deficiency:
- Slow wound healing and frequent infections
- Skin problems including acne, eczema, or dermatitis
- Hair loss or changes in hair texture
- Loss of taste or smell sensitivity
- White spots on fingernails
- Mood changes including depression or irritability

• Copper's Critical Functions:
- Required for superoxide dismutase, a crucial antioxidant enzyme
- Necessary for collagen and elastin formation
- Supports iron absorption and utilization
- Required for neurotransmitter synthesis
- Essential for melanin production and skin pigmentation

• Signs of Copper Deficiency:
- Premature graying of hair
- Skin that bruises easily or heals poorly
- Fatigue that doesn't improve with iron supplementation
- Frequent infections or poor immune function
- Joint pain or connective tissue problems
- Neurological symptoms including numbness or tingling

➢ Balancing Zinc and Copper Through Food

• High-Quality Zinc Sources:
- Oysters and other shellfish (also provide copper in proper ratios)
- Grass-fed beef and lamb
- Pumpkin seeds and hemp seeds
- Dark chocolate and cacao
- Tahini and sesame seeds

• Copper-Rich Foods:
- Organ meats, particularly liver
- Shellfish and seafood
- Nuts, especially cashews and Brazil nuts

- Seeds, particularly sunflower seeds
- Dark leafy greens
- Mushrooms, especially shiitake

• Strategic Food Combinations:
- Consume oysters regularly for optimal zinc-copper ratios
- Include organ meats weekly if tolerated
- Combine zinc-rich seeds with copper-rich nuts
- Balance meat consumption with copper-rich vegetables
- Avoid zinc supplements without corresponding copper intake

The Magnesium-Calcium Partnership: Muscle Relaxation and Nervous System Calm

The relationship between magnesium and calcium affects every cell in your body, with particular importance for inflammatory regulation, muscle function, and nervous system health.

The Modern Calcium-Magnesium Imbalance

Most people consume far too much calcium relative to magnesium, creating ratios that promote inflammation, muscle tension, and nervous system hyperactivity. The optimal calcium-to-magnesium ratio ranges from 1:1 to 2:1, but typical Western diets provide ratios of 5:1 or higher.

➢ Magnesium's Anti-Inflammatory Functions:
- Regulates over 300 enzymatic reactions involved in inflammatory control
- Supports muscle relaxation and prevents inflammatory muscle tension
- Stabilizes nervous system function and stress responses
- Required for energy production in every cell
- Supports healthy sleep patterns and stress recovery
- Necessary for vitamin D activation and bone health

Signs of Magnesium Deficiency:
- Muscle cramps, twitches, or tension
- Difficulty falling asleep or staying asleep
- Anxiety, irritability, or mood swings

- Headaches or migraines
- Constipation or digestive issues
- Chocolate cravings (the body's attempt to obtain magnesium)
- Fatigue that doesn't improve with rest

➢ Calcium's Proper Role:
When balanced with adequate magnesium, calcium supports:
- Bone and tooth structure
- Muscle contraction and nerve transmission
- Blood clotting and wound healing
- Cellular communication and signaling

Problems with Excess Calcium:
- Muscle cramps and tension
- Kidney stone formation
- Arterial calcification and cardiovascular problems
- Interference with magnesium and other mineral absorption
- Increased inflammatory responses

Optimizing Magnesium-Calcium Balance

➢ High-Quality Magnesium Sources:
- Dark leafy greens (spinach, Swiss chard, kale)
- Nuts and seeds (almonds, pumpkin seeds, hemp seeds)
- Dark chocolate and cacao
- Avocados and bananas
- Whole grains (quinoa, brown rice, oats)
- Legumes (black beans, lentils, chickpeas)

➢ Balanced Calcium Sources:
- Leafy greens (provide both calcium and magnesium)
- Sesame seeds and tahini
- Sardines and canned salmon with bones
- Almonds and other nuts
- Fermented dairy products if tolerated

➢ Absorption Enhancement Strategies:
- Consume magnesium-rich foods throughout the day rather than in large doses
- Include vitamin D-rich foods to support calcium absorption
- Avoid consuming calcium-rich foods with iron-rich meals
- Include vitamin K2-rich foods (fermented foods, grass-fed dairy) to direct calcium to bones rather than soft tissues

- Consume magnesium-rich foods in the evening to support sleep and muscle relaxation

The Sodium-Potassium Balance: Fluid Regulation and Inflammatory Control

The sodium-potassium ratio significantly affects fluid balance, blood pressure, and inflammatory responses throughout your body.

The Modern Sodium-Potassium Crisis

Processed foods have created a dramatic reversal in the natural sodium-potassium ratio. Our ancestors consumed roughly 16 times more potassium than sodium, while modern diets often provide more sodium than potassium—a complete inversion that promotes inflammation and chronic disease.

➤ Potassium's Anti-Inflammatory Benefits:
- Supports healthy blood pressure and cardiovascular function
- Regulates fluid balance and reduces inflammatory edema
- Required for proper muscle and nerve function
- Supports kidney function and toxin elimination
- Helps maintain proper pH balance in body fluids

Signs of Potassium Deficiency:
- Muscle weakness or cramping
- Fatigue and low energy
- Irregular heartbeat or palpitations
- High blood pressure
- Kidney stones
- Salt cravings

Strategic Sodium-Potassium Optimization:

➤ High-Potassium Foods:
- Leafy greens (spinach, kale, Swiss chard)
- Avocados and bananas
- Sweet potatoes and winter squash
- White beans and lentils
- Salmon and other fish
- Coconut water and vegetable juices

➤ Sodium Reduction Strategies:
- Eliminate processed and packaged foods
- Use herbs and spices instead of salt for flavoring
- Choose fresh foods over canned or preserved options
- Read labels carefully and avoid high-sodium products
- Use sea salt or Himalayan salt in small amounts when needed

The Forgotten Anti-Inflammatory Trio: Betaine, Taurine, and Glycine

Three amino acids and amino acid derivatives provide powerful anti-inflammatory benefits but rarely receive attention in mainstream nutritional discussions. These compounds support fundamental cellular processes that control inflammatory responses.

Betaine: The Methylation and Osmolyte Master

Betaine, also known as trimethylglycine, serves dual functions in your body: supporting methylation reactions crucial for inflammatory control and acting as an osmolyte that protects cells from stress.

➤ Betaine's Anti-Inflammatory Mechanisms:
- Supports methylation reactions that control gene expression and inflammatory responses
- Protects cells from osmotic stress and inflammatory damage
- Supports liver detoxification and fat metabolism
- Reduces homocysteine levels, decreasing cardiovascular inflammation
- Supports muscle protein synthesis and exercise recovery

➤ Natural Betaine Sources:
- Beets and beet greens (highest concentration)
- Spinach and other leafy greens
- Quinoa and amaranth
- Sweet potatoes
- Turkey and other poultry
- Shellfish, particularly shrimp and crab

➤ Maximizing Betaine Benefits:

- Include beets or beet juice regularly in your diet
- Consume betaine-rich foods with meals to support digestion
- Combine with B-vitamins to enhance methylation support
- Include both the root and greens of beets for maximum betaine content

Taurine: The Cellular Protector and Nervous System Calmer

Taurine represents one of the most abundant amino acids in your body, with particularly high concentrations in your heart, brain, and muscles. This compound provides multiple anti-inflammatory benefits while supporting cellular protection and nervous system function.

➤ Taurine's Anti-Inflammatory Actions:
- Stabilizes cell membranes and prevents inflammatory damage
- Supports healthy calcium handling in cells
- Acts as an antioxidant and supports other antioxidant systems
- Modulates inflammatory cytokine production
- Supports healthy blood pressure and cardiovascular function
- Calms nervous system activity and supports stress resilience

➤ Natural Taurine Sources:
- Fish and seafood (particularly high in shellfish)
- Poultry, especially dark meat
- Organ meats
- Eggs
- Dairy products
- Seaweed and sea vegetables

Note: Plant foods contain minimal taurine, making this nutrient particularly important for people following plant-based diets.

➤ Taurine Optimization Strategies:
- Include fish or seafood several times per week
- Choose dark meat poultry over white meat
- Include organ meats if tolerated
- Consider taurine supplementation if following a plant-based diet
- Support taurine synthesis with adequate B-vitamins and zinc

Glycine: The Collagen Builder and Sleep Supporter

Glycine serves as the simplest amino acid but provides complex anti-inflammatory benefits throughout your body. This amino acid supports collagen production, sleep quality, and inflammatory resolution.

➤ Glycine's Anti-Inflammatory Functions:
- Required for collagen synthesis and tissue repair
- Supports glutathione production and detoxification
- Modulates inflammatory cytokine responses
- Supports healthy sleep patterns and stress recovery
- Balances methionine metabolism and prevents inflammatory metabolites
- Supports digestive health and gut barrier function

➤ Natural Glycine Sources:
- Bone broth and gelatin
- Collagen-rich cuts of meat
- Fish and seafood
- Poultry skin and cartilage
- Organ meats
- Eggs, particularly the whites

➤ Glycine Enhancement Strategies:
- Include bone broth regularly in your diet
- Choose collagen-rich cuts of meat over lean muscle meat exclusively
- Include gelatin or collagen supplements if whole food sources are insufficient
- Consume glycine-rich foods in the evening to support sleep
- Balance high-methionine foods (muscle meats) with glycine-rich options

Creating Your Complete Anti-Inflammatory Nutrient Strategy

Understanding individual nutrients and their interactions allows you to create a comprehensive anti-inflammatory nutrition strategy that goes far beyond basic omega-3 supplementation.

Daily Anti-Inflammatory Nutrient Checklist:

➢ Polyphenol Diversity:
- Multiple colors of vegetables and fruits
- Fresh herbs and spices with each meal
- Green tea or other polyphenol-rich beverages
- Strategic combinations for enhanced absorption

➢ Sulfur Compound Support:
- At least one serving of cruciferous vegetables
- Fresh garlic or onions with meals
- Adequate sulfur amino acids from protein sources
- Support nutrients for sulfur metabolism

➢ Mineral Balance Optimization:
- Zinc-rich foods balanced with copper sources
- Magnesium-rich foods throughout the day
- Potassium-rich vegetables with minimal processed sodium
- Strategic mineral combinations for enhanced absorption

➢ Forgotten Nutrient Integration:
- Betaine-rich foods for methylation support
- Taurine sources for cellular protection
- Glycine-rich foods for tissue repair and sleep support
- Balance between all amino acids for optimal utilization

Weekly Anti-Inflammatory Menu Planning:

➢ Daily Non-Negotiables:
- Colorful vegetables with every meal
- Fresh herbs or spices with each dish
- High-quality protein sources with complementary nutrients
- Mineral-rich foods balanced throughout the day

➢ Weekly Targets:
- Fish or seafood 3-4 times per week for taurine and omega-3s
- Organ meats or shellfish once per week for zinc-copper balance
- Bone broth or collagen-rich foods several times per week for glycine
- Variety of cruciferous vegetables for sulfur compound diversity

This comprehensive approach to anti-inflammatory nutrition provides the foundation for lasting improvements in inflammatory status. By understanding how nutrients work together synergistically, you can create powerful anti-inflammatory effects through strategic food choices rather than relying on isolated supplements or single-nutrient approaches.

Chapter 4

Biohacking Your Anti-Inflammatory Response

Your body generates measurable signals that reveal your inflammatory status in real-time. By learning to read these signals and strategically manipulate your environment, you can optimize your anti-inflammatory response with precision that goes far beyond dietary changes alone. This chapter will teach you how to become your own inflammation detective, using simple biohacking tools and techniques to accelerate your healing and maintain optimal inflammatory balance.

Modern biohacking doesn't require expensive equipment or laboratory access. The most powerful tools for monitoring and optimizing your inflammatory response are available to you right now, often using nothing more than your smartphone and basic household items. What matters is understanding which signals to track and how to interpret them in the context of your unique inflammatory fingerprint.

Using Heart Rate Variability to Monitor Your Inflammatory Status

Your heart doesn't beat like a metronome. Instead, it constantly adjusts its rhythm in response to your nervous system's demands, creating subtle variations between heartbeats that reveal profound information about your body's internal state. This heart rate variability (HRV) serves as a real-time window into your autonomic nervous system and, by extension, your inflammatory status.

Understanding HRV as Your Inflammatory Dashboard

Heart rate variability reflects the balance between your sympathetic nervous system (your body's "fight or flight" response) and your parasympathetic nervous system (your "rest and digest" response). When inflammation is present in your body, it shifts this balance toward sympathetic dominance, reducing your HRV and indicating that your body is under stress.

Think of HRV as your body's internal stress meter. Higher HRV generally indicates that your nervous system is resilient and adaptive, suggesting lower inflammatory burden and better recovery capacity. Lower HRV suggests that your body is dealing with stressors—whether physical, emotional, or inflammatory—that are taxing your adaptive capacity.

What Your HRV Numbers Mean:

Your baseline HRV depends on your age, fitness level, and individual physiology, but the trends matter more than absolute numbers. A declining HRV trend over several days indicates increasing stress or inflammatory burden, while improving HRV suggests your anti-inflammatory strategies are working.

Daily HRV Interpretation:
- Green Zone (Above your baseline): Your body is recovered and ready for stress or training
- Yellow Zone (Near your baseline): Moderate stress or inflammation present, proceed with caution
- Red Zone (Below your baseline): High stress or inflammatory burden, focus on recovery

Practical HRV Monitoring for Inflammation Management

You can monitor your HRV using smartphone apps like HRV4Training, Elite HRV, or Welltory, along with a chest strap heart rate monitor or quality fitness tracker. The key is consistency—measure at the same time each day, preferably upon waking before getting out of bed.

Your Daily HRV Protocol:

1. Measure upon waking: Take your HRV reading before checking your phone, getting up, or drinking water

2. Record contextual factors: Note your sleep quality, stress level, previous day's activities, and any symptoms
3. Track dietary experiments: Monitor how different foods affect your HRV over 24-48 hours
4. Identify patterns: Look for correlations between your HRV and inflammatory symptoms
5. Adjust your day accordingly: Use your HRV reading to guide your stress exposure and recovery activities

Using HRV to Test Anti-Inflammatory Interventions:

Your HRV provides objective feedback about the effectiveness of your anti-inflammatory strategies. Here's how to use it systematically:

➢ Testing New Foods:
- Establish a 3-day baseline HRV before introducing a new food
- Monitor HRV for 3 days after introducing the food
- Compare the averages to determine if the food is inflammatory for you
- Look for delayed responses, as some foods affect HRV 12-24 hours after consumption

➢ Evaluating Lifestyle Changes:
- Track HRV before and after implementing new sleep schedules
- Monitor the impact of different exercise intensities on your recovery
- Assess how stress management techniques affect your autonomic balance
- Evaluate the inflammatory impact of environmental changes

HRV Red Flags That Indicate Inflammatory Burden:

Certain HRV patterns consistently indicate increased inflammatory activity:
- Sudden drops in HRV without obvious cause
- HRV that remains suppressed for multiple consecutive days
- HRV that doesn't improve with rest and recovery
- Wide fluctuations in HRV from day to day
- HRV that decreases after meals (indicating food sensitivities)

Advanced HRV Analysis for Inflammatory Optimization

Once you've mastered basic HRV monitoring, you can use more sophisticated analysis to fine-tune your anti-inflammatory approach.

Weekly HRV Trends:

Look at your weekly HRV average and trend:
- Improving trend: Your anti-inflammatory strategies are working
- Stable trend: You've reached a plateau and may need to adjust your approach
- Declining trend: Inflammatory burden is increasing or you're overreaching

HRV Recovery Patterns:

Monitor how quickly your HRV returns to baseline after different stressors:
- Fast recovery (1-2 days): Good inflammatory resilience
- Slow recovery (3-5 days): Moderate inflammatory burden or poor recovery capacity
- No recovery (>5 days): High inflammatory burden requiring immediate attention

Seasonal HRV Variations:

Your HRV naturally fluctuates with seasonal changes, daylight exposure, and environmental factors. Understanding these patterns helps you distinguish between normal variations and inflammatory responses:
- Winter typically shows lower HRV due to reduced daylight and increased stress
- Spring often brings HRV improvements as daylight increases
- Summer may show variable HRV due to heat stress and travel
- Fall frequently demonstrates stable HRV as routines normalize

Cold and Heat Therapy Integration with Dietary Changes

Temperature therapy represents one of the most powerful biohacking tools for modulating inflammation. Both cold and heat exposure trigger specific physiological responses that can either enhance or complement your dietary anti-inflammatory strategies. The key lies in understanding when and how to use each modality for maximum benefit.

Cold Therapy: Harnessing Controlled Stress for Anti-Inflammatory Benefits

Cold exposure creates a controlled stress that stimulates your body's adaptive responses, including enhanced anti-inflammatory pathways. Regular cold therapy can improve your inflammatory resilience, boost immune function, and accelerate recovery from inflammatory episodes.

The Science Behind Cold-Induced Anti-Inflammatory Effects:

When you expose your body to cold, several beneficial processes occur:
- Activation of brown adipose tissue, which produces anti-inflammatory compounds
- Stimulation of the vagus nerve, promoting parasympathetic recovery
- Release of norepinephrine, which has anti-inflammatory effects at appropriate levels
- Improved circulation and lymphatic drainage
- Enhanced mitochondrial function and cellular energy production

Progressive Cold Therapy Protocol:

Start conservatively and build tolerance gradually to avoid overwhelming your system:

➢ Week 1-2: Foundation Phase
- End your regular shower with 30 seconds of cold water
- Focus on controlled breathing and relaxation during cold exposure
- Gradually extend to 60 seconds as tolerance improves
- Monitor your HRV response to gauge your body's adaptation

➢ Week 3-4: Building Phase
- Extend cold shower duration to 2-3 minutes
- Experiment with cold water face immersion for 30 seconds

- Consider ice baths or cold plunge pools if available
- Track energy levels and inflammatory symptoms

➢ Week 5+: Optimization Phase
- Develop a consistent cold therapy routine 3-4 times per week
- Experiment with different temperatures and durations
- Integrate cold therapy timing with your meal schedule
- Use cold therapy strategically for inflammatory flare-ups

Timing Cold Therapy with Your Anti-Inflammatory Diet:

The timing of cold exposure relative to your meals can significantly impact its effectiveness:

➢ Pre-meal Cold Therapy (30-60 minutes before eating):
- Activates brown fat and improves insulin sensitivity
- Enhances nutrient uptake and utilization
- Particularly beneficial before meals higher in carbohydrates
- Can help mitigate inflammatory responses to imperfect food choices

➢ Post-meal Cold Therapy (2-3 hours after eating):
- Aids in digestion and reduces post-meal inflammation
- Helps manage blood sugar spikes from meals
- Particularly useful after larger or more indulgent meals
- Should be avoided immediately after eating to prevent digestive disruption

➢ Fasting Cold Therapy:
- Maximizes fat burning and ketone production
- Enhances autophagy and cellular cleanup processes
- Amplifies the anti-inflammatory benefits of intermittent fasting
- Best performed during the latter half of your fasting window

Heat Therapy: Deep Tissue Anti-Inflammatory Recovery

Heat therapy works through different mechanisms than cold therapy, promoting deep relaxation, improved circulation, and activation of heat shock proteins that protect against inflammatory damage. Sauna use, in particular, has been extensively studied for its anti-inflammatory benefits.

The Anti-Inflammatory Mechanisms of Heat Therapy:

Regular heat exposure provides multiple anti-inflammatory benefits:
- Activation of heat shock proteins that protect cells from stress
- Improved cardiovascular function and circulation
- Enhanced lymphatic drainage and toxin elimination
- Deep muscle relaxation and tension release
- Stimulation of endorphin release for mood and pain relief

Progressive Heat Therapy Protocol:

Build heat tolerance gradually while monitoring your body's response:

➤ Beginner Protocol (Weeks 1-2):
- 10-15 minutes in a sauna at 160-170°F (70-75°C)
- 2-3 sessions per week
- Focus on proper hydration before, during, and after sessions
- Exit if you feel dizzy, nauseous, or uncomfortable

➤ Intermediate Protocol (Weeks 3-4):
- 15-20 minutes in a sauna at 170-180°F (75-80°C)
- 3-4 sessions per week
- Experiment with contrast therapy (alternating hot and cold)
- Monitor HRV response to gauge recovery

➤ Advanced Protocol (Week 5+):
- 20-30 minutes in a sauna at 180-190°F (80-85°C)
- 4-5 sessions per week
- Integrate infrared sauna if available for deeper tissue penetration
- Use heat therapy strategically for inflammatory conditions

Optimizing Heat Therapy Timing:

The timing of heat therapy relative to meals and other activities affects its anti-inflammatory impact:

➤ Pre-workout Heat Therapy:
- Light heat exposure (10-15 minutes) can enhance flexibility and reduce injury risk
- Improves blood flow to muscles and joints
- Should be followed by adequate cool-down before intense exercise

➤ Post-workout Heat Therapy:
- 15-20 minutes of heat therapy aids muscle recovery
- Helps reduce post-exercise inflammation
- Should be delayed at least 30 minutes after intense exercise
- Combines well with hydration and electrolyte replacement

➤ Evening Heat Therapy:
- Promotes relaxation and prepares the body for sleep
- Timing should allow body temperature to normalize before bed (2-3 hours)
- Can be combined with meditation or gentle stretching
- Particularly beneficial for stress-related inflammation

Contrast Therapy: Maximizing Anti-Inflammatory Benefits

Alternating between hot and cold exposure, known as contrast therapy, can amplify the anti-inflammatory benefits of temperature therapy. This technique stimulates circulation, enhances lymphatic drainage, and provides a powerful stimulus for adaptive responses.

Contrast Therapy Protocol:

➢ Basic Contrast Shower:
- 3 minutes hot water (as hot as comfortably tolerable)
- 1 minute cold water (as cold as available)
- Repeat 3-4 cycles
- Always end with cold water
- Perform 2-3 times per week

➢ Advanced Contrast Protocol:
- 15 minutes sauna followed by 2-3 minutes cold plunge
- Repeat 2-3 cycles
- Rest 5-10 minutes between cycles
- Hydrate adequately throughout the process
- Monitor HRV response for 24-48 hours after sessions

Exercise Timing and Intensity for Optimal Inflammatory Response

Exercise represents both a pro-inflammatory and anti-inflammatory stimulus, depending on the timing, intensity, and your current inflammatory status. Understanding how to optimize your exercise approach based on your inflammatory state can dramatically improve your results while preventing overtraining and inflammatory flare-ups.

All exercise creates some degree of inflammation as part of the adaptive process. This acute inflammatory response is necessary for improvements in strength, endurance, and overall fitness. However, when exercise is poorly timed or excessive in intensity, it can contribute to chronic inflammatory burden rather than inflammatory resilience.

The Exercise Inflammation Curve:

Your inflammatory response to exercise follows a predictable pattern:
- Immediate response (0-6 hours): Acute inflammatory markers rise
- Peak inflammation (6-24 hours): Maximum inflammatory response occurs
- Resolution phase (24-72 hours): Anti-inflammatory processes predominate
- Adaptation phase (72+ hours): Improved inflammatory resilience develops

The key to optimizing exercise for anti-inflammatory benefits lies in ensuring complete progression through this cycle before applying the next exercise stimulus.

Using HRV to Guide Exercise Intensity

Your HRV provides real-time feedback about your body's readiness for exercise stress and its ability to handle inflammatory challenges. This objective data allows you to optimize your training for maximum anti-inflammatory benefit.

HRV-Guided Exercise Protocols:

➢ High HRV Days (Green Zone):
- Your body is recovered and ready for higher intensity exercise
- Suitable for strength training, high-intensity intervals, or longer endurance sessions
- Can handle multiple exercise stressors in the same day
- Good time to push your limits or try new training modalities

➢ Moderate HRV Days (Yellow Zone):
- Your body is managing some stress or inflammatory burden
- Focus on moderate intensity, steady-state exercise
- Avoid high-intensity intervals or maximum effort training
- Consider yoga, walking, or light resistance training

➢ Low HRV Days (Red Zone):
- Your body is dealing with significant stress or inflammation
- Prioritize gentle movement and recovery activities
- Walking, stretching, or restorative yoga are appropriate
- Avoid intense exercise that could worsen inflammatory burden

Timing Exercise with Your Anti-Inflammatory Diet

The timing of exercise relative to your meals significantly affects both exercise performance and inflammatory response. Strategic timing can enhance the anti-inflammatory benefits of both exercise and nutrition.

Pre-Exercise Nutrition for Anti-Inflammatory Benefits:

➢ Fasted Exercise (12+ hours since last meal):
- Maximizes fat burning and ketone production
- Enhances autophagy and cellular cleanup processes
- Reduces exercise-induced oxidative stress
- Best for low-to-moderate intensity, shorter duration exercise
- Requires adequate hydration and electrolyte balance

➢ Pre-Exercise Anti-Inflammatory Fuel (1-2 hours before exercise):
- Small amount of easily digestible carbohydrates with anti-inflammatory foods
- Examples: berries with coconut oil, green tea with raw honey
- Provides energy while supporting anti-inflammatory pathways
- Suitable for moderate-to-high intensity exercise

Post-Exercise Recovery Nutrition:

The post-exercise window represents a critical opportunity to support recovery and minimize inflammatory damage:

➢ Immediate Post-Exercise (0-30 minutes):
- Focus on hydration and electrolyte replacement
- Consider anti-inflammatory compounds like tart cherry juice or turmeric
- Avoid large meals immediately after intense exercise
- Light, easily digestible options if hungry

➢ Recovery Meal (1-2 hours post-exercise):
- Combine high-quality protein with anti-inflammatory carbohydrates
- Include omega-3 fatty acids to support resolution of exercise-induced inflammation
- Examples: wild salmon with sweet potato, grass-fed beef with quinoa and vegetables
- Time this meal to support overnight recovery processes

Optimizing Exercise Timing for Circadian Anti-Inflammatory Rhythms

Your body's inflammatory processes follow circadian rhythms, with natural peaks and valleys throughout the day. Aligning your exercise timing with these rhythms can optimize both performance and anti-inflammatory benefits.

Morning Exercise (6-10 AM):

➢ Benefits:
- Aligns with natural cortisol peak for optimal energy
- Enhances insulin sensitivity throughout the day
- Supports healthy circadian rhythm regulation
- Maximizes post-exercise metabolic benefits

➢ Considerations:
- Allow adequate warm-up time as body temperature is lower
- Ensure proper hydration after overnight fasting
- Consider light pre-exercise fuel if training intensity is high
- Monitor HRV as morning readings may be more variable

Afternoon Exercise (2-6 PM):

➢ Benefits:
- Body temperature is naturally higher, reducing injury risk
- Perceived exertion is typically lower
- Good compromise between morning and evening benefits
- Allows for proper pre-exercise nutrition

➢ Considerations:
- May interfere with work schedules
- Requires planning for pre and post-exercise nutrition
- Can be affected by accumulated daily stress
- Monitor caffeine intake if exercising later in this window

Evening Exercise (6-8 PM):

➢ Benefits:
- Can serve as stress relief from daily pressures
- Body temperature and flexibility are typically optimal

- Good option for strength training and skill-based activities

➢ Considerations:
- Must be completed early enough to allow body temperature to normalize before bed
- Post-exercise meal timing becomes critical for sleep quality
- May interfere with evening recovery and relaxation routines
- Avoid within 3 hours of bedtime to prevent sleep disruption

Exercise Intensity Periodization for Inflammatory Management

Rather than maintaining consistent exercise intensity, periodizing your training based on your inflammatory status and life circumstances can optimize long-term benefits while preventing overtraining.

Weekly Periodization Model:

➢ Monday: Assessment and Planning
- Check HRV and inflammatory symptoms
- Plan the week's exercise based on your current status
- Schedule higher intensity sessions for days when HRV is optimal
- Build in flexibility for adjustments based on daily HRV readings

➢ Tuesday-Thursday: Primary Training Days
- Focus on your most important or intense training sessions
- Take advantage of mid-week energy and recovery capacity
- Monitor HRV daily to ensure adequate recovery between sessions

➢ Friday: Moderate Intensity
- Transition toward weekend recovery
- Good day for skill-based or enjoyable activities
- Avoid high-intensity sessions that might impair weekend recovery

➢ Weekend: Recovery and Restoration
- Prioritize gentle movement and recovery activities

- Focus on activities that reduce stress and promote relaxation
- Use this time for longer, lower-intensity activities like hiking or swimming

Monthly Periodization for Inflammatory Resilience:

➢ Week 1: Foundation Building
- Establish consistent exercise routine
- Focus on proper form and technique
- Build aerobic base with moderate intensity

➢ Week 2: Intensity Introduction
- Add higher intensity intervals
- Increase training volume gradually
- Monitor recovery carefully

➢ Week 3: Peak Training
- Highest intensity and volume of the month
- Push limits while maintaining proper recovery
- This week tests your inflammatory resilience

➢ Week 4: Recovery and Adaptation
- Reduce intensity and volume significantly
- Focus on recovery activities and restoration
- Allow adaptations to occur and inflammatory balance to restore

Sleep Optimization Strategies That Complement Dietary Changes

Sleep represents your body's primary opportunity to resolve inflammation and repair damage accumulated during waking hours. However, sleep optimization goes far beyond simply getting more hours in bed. The quality, timing, and environmental conditions of your sleep dramatically affect your body's ability to manage inflammation effectively.

During sleep, your body activates powerful anti-inflammatory and repair processes that are largely suppressed during waking hours. Understanding these mechanisms allows you to optimize your sleep environment and habits for maximum anti-inflammatory benefit.

The Glymphatic System: Your Brain's Overnight Cleanup Crew

Your brain contains a specialized system called the glymphatic system that becomes highly active during deep sleep. This system flushes inflammatory waste products, including amyloid beta and tau proteins associated with neurodegeneration, from your brain tissue.

The glymphatic system works most effectively when:
- You achieve adequate deep sleep stages
- You sleep on your side rather than your back or stomach
- You maintain proper hydration without overhydrating before bed
- Your bedroom temperature is cool (65-68°F)
- You avoid alcohol and substances that suppress deep sleep

Growth Hormone and Tissue Repair

Your body produces the majority of its growth hormone during deep sleep, particularly during the first half of the night. Growth hormone drives tissue repair, muscle recovery, and anti-inflammatory processes throughout your body.

Optimizing growth hormone production requires:
- Consistent sleep timing, especially going to bed before 11 PM
- Avoiding large meals within 3 hours of bedtime
- Maintaining stable blood sugar throughout the night
- Ensuring adequate magnesium and zinc intake
- Creating complete darkness in your sleep environment

Sleep Timing Optimization for Anti-Inflammatory Benefits

The timing of your sleep, not just its duration, significantly affects your body's inflammatory processes. Your circadian rhythms coordinate inflammatory and anti-inflammatory activities throughout the 24-hour cycle.

The Anti-Inflammatory Sleep Window:

Your body's anti-inflammatory processes are most active between 10 PM and 2 AM. Missing this window, even if you sleep the same total

hours, reduces the anti-inflammatory benefits of sleep.

Optimal Sleep Schedule:
- 10 PM - 6 AM: Aligns with natural circadian rhythms
- 9:30 PM - 5:30 AM: Good for early risers
- 10:30 PM - 6:30 AM: Acceptable for night owls
- 11 PM - 7 AM: Minimum effective timing for most people

➢ Signs Your Sleep Timing Needs Adjustment:
- Difficulty falling asleep despite being tired
- Waking up groggy even after adequate sleep hours
- Afternoon energy crashes
- Increased cravings for inflammatory foods
- Declining HRV trends despite good lifestyle habits

Creating Your Anti-Inflammatory Sleep Environment

Your sleep environment significantly affects your body's ability to activate anti-inflammatory processes. Small changes to your bedroom can dramatically improve sleep quality and inflammatory recovery.

Temperature Optimization:

Your core body temperature naturally drops during sleep, triggering anti-inflammatory processes. Supporting this natural temperature decline enhances sleep quality:

- Maintain bedroom temperature between 65-68°F (18-20°C)
- Use breathable, natural fiber bedding
- Consider cooling mattress toppers or chilipads for hot sleepers
- Take a warm bath 90 minutes before bed to accelerate cooling
- Wear minimal, loose-fitting sleepwear

Light Environment Management:

Light exposure affects melatonin production and circadian rhythm regulation, directly impacting inflammatory processes:

➢ Evening Light Protocol:
- Dim lights progressively after sunset
- Use warm, amber lighting instead of bright white lights
- Avoid screens within 2 hours of bedtime, or use blue light blocking glasses
- Consider salt lamps or candles for evening ambiance
- Install blackout curtains or use a high-quality sleep mask

➢ Morning Light Protocol:
- Expose yourself to bright light within 30 minutes of waking
- Spend 10-15 minutes outdoors in natural sunlight
- Use a light therapy lamp during winter months or if natural light is limited
- Keep bedroom curtains open to allow natural light awakening when possible

Nutrition Timing for Optimal Sleep and Anti-Inflammatory Recovery

The timing and composition of your meals significantly affect sleep quality and overnight anti-inflammatory processes. Strategic nutrition timing can enhance both sleep and inflammatory recovery.

Pre-Sleep Nutrition Guidelines:

➢ 3-4 Hours Before Bed: Last Large Meal
- Complete digestion of substantial meals before sleep
- Include foods that support serotonin and melatonin production
- Examples: wild salmon with sweet potato, turkey with quinoa
- Avoid spicy, acidic, or highly processed foods

➢ 2 Hours Before Bed: Light Snack (if needed)
- Small portion of easily digestible, sleep-promoting foods
- Focus on foods that stabilize blood sugar overnight
- Examples: handful of almonds, small apple with almond butter, herbal tea with raw honey
- Avoid caffeine, alcohol, and high-sugar foods

➢ 1 Hour Before Bed: Hydration Cutoff
- Complete most hydration needs by this time
- Small sips of water acceptable if thirsty
- Avoid large amounts of fluid that might disrupt sleep
- Consider magnesium supplementation if appropriate

Sleep-Promoting Anti-Inflammatory Foods:

Certain foods contain compounds that support both sleep quality and anti-inflammatory processes:

➢ Tryptophan-Rich Foods:
- Turkey, chicken, eggs, salmon
- Pumpkin seeds, sesame seeds, walnuts
- Tart cherries (natural source of melatonin)
- Combine with complex carbohydrates for optimal uptake

➢ Magnesium-Rich Foods:
- Dark leafy greens, avocados, nuts, seeds
- Dark chocolate (in small amounts)
- Epsom salt baths for transdermal absorption
- Supports muscle relaxation and nervous system calming

➢ Anti-Inflammatory Herbs and Spices:
- Turmeric with black pepper (consume earlier in evening)
- Ginger tea for digestive support
- Chamomile tea for relaxation
- Passionflower or valerian root (if tolerated)

Advanced Sleep Optimization Techniques

Once you've mastered the fundamentals of sleep hygiene, advanced techniques can further enhance your sleep's anti-inflammatory benefits.

Sleep Position Optimization:

Your sleep position affects lymphatic drainage and inflammatory waste removal:
- Side sleeping (particularly left side) optimizes glymphatic function
- Elevate your head slightly to promote lymphatic drainage
- Use a pillow between your knees to maintain spinal alignment

- Avoid stomach sleeping, which can impair breathing and circulation

Breathing Optimization:

Your breathing patterns during sleep affect oxygenation and nervous system activation:
- Practice nasal breathing exercises before bed
- Consider mouth taping (with appropriate tape) if you're a mouth breather
- Address sleep apnea or breathing disorders that disrupt sleep architecture
- Use a humidifier to maintain optimal nasal breathing conditions

Sleep Tracking and Optimization:

Use technology to monitor and optimize your sleep for anti-inflammatory benefits:
- Track sleep stages to ensure adequate deep sleep
- Monitor HRV during sleep to assess recovery quality
- Use smart alarm clocks that wake you during lighter sleep stages
- Correlate sleep metrics with daily inflammatory symptoms and HRV readings

Recovery Week Sleep Protocols:

Periodically implement intensive sleep recovery protocols:
- Extend sleep duration by 1-2 hours for 7-10 days
- Maintain strict sleep hygiene during recovery periods
- Focus on maximizing deep sleep through environmental optimization
- Monitor improvements in HRV, energy, and inflammatory symptoms

Integrating Your Biohacking Protocols

The true power of biohacking your anti-inflammatory response lies in integrating these various approaches into a cohesive system that works synergistically. Your HRV monitoring provides the feedback loop that allows you to adjust your cold therapy, heat therapy, exercise, and sleep protocols based on your body's actual responses.

Daily Integration Protocol:

➢ Morning:
- Check HRV upon waking
- Adjust exercise intensity based on HRV reading
- Consider cold therapy before breakfast to enhance metabolic benefits
- Expose yourself to natural light to support circadian rhythms

➢ Afternoon:
- Time exercise based on HRV and energy levels
- Use heat therapy post-workout for recovery
- Monitor stress levels and implement stress reduction techniques as needed

➢ Evening:
- Optimize pre-sleep nutrition timing
- Create ideal sleep environment
- Consider gentle heat therapy (warm bath) to promote relaxation
- Practice breathing exercises or meditation to prepare for sleep

Weekly Integration Cycle:

➢ High HRV Days:
- Implement more intense exercise protocols
- Use contrast therapy (hot/cold) for maximum adaptation
- Push boundaries with biohacking experiments
- Focus on building resilience and capacity

➢ Low HRV Days:
- Prioritize gentle movement and recovery
- Use heat therapy for relaxation and stress relief
- Focus on sleep optimization and stress reduction
- Avoid additional stressors or intense biohacking protocols

By systematically implementing these biohacking strategies while monitoring your body's responses through HRV and symptom tracking, you can optimize your anti-inflammatory response with precision and achieve results that go far beyond dietary changes alone. The key is consistency, patience, and careful attention to your body's feedback signals.

Chapter 5

Environmental Factors That Sabotage Progress

You've cleaned up your diet, improved your sleep, and managed your stress—yet you're still experiencing inflammatory symptoms that seem to come and go without explanation. The missing piece of your anti-inflammatory puzzle may be hiding in plain sight throughout your daily environment. From the air you breathe in your home to the electromagnetic fields surrounding your devices, environmental factors can silently trigger inflammation and undermine even the most perfect dietary protocol.

Environmental inflammation represents one of the most overlooked aspects of chronic inflammatory conditions. Unlike dietary triggers that produce relatively predictable responses, environmental inflammatory triggers operate subtly, often causing delayed reactions that make them difficult to identify. However, once you understand how to recognize and address these hidden saboteurs, you can eliminate major barriers to your healing progress.

Hidden Inflammatory Triggers in Your Home Environment

Your home should be your sanctuary from inflammatory stress, yet modern homes often harbor multiple sources of chronic inflammatory exposure. These environmental triggers work synergistically with dietary and lifestyle factors, creating a total inflammatory load that can overwhelm your body's natural resolution mechanisms.

The Indoor Air Quality Crisis

The air inside your home is typically 2-5 times more polluted than outdoor air, and in some cases up to 100 times more contaminated. This indoor air pollution creates a constant source of inflammatory stress that affects every breath you take, 24 hours a day.

Volatile Organic Compounds (VOCs): The Silent Inflammatory Triggers

VOCs are chemicals that easily evaporate at room temperature, creating invisible clouds of inflammatory compounds throughout your home. These chemicals trigger inflammatory responses in your respiratory system, skin, and nervous system, often causing symptoms that seem unrelated to air quality.

Common sources of VOCs in your home include:
- New furniture, carpets, and building materials that "off-gas" chemicals
- Cleaning products, air fresheners, and personal care items
- Paint, varnishes, and adhesives
- Dry cleaning chemicals and fabric treatments
- Candles and incense, particularly those with synthetic fragrances

Identifying VOC Exposure in Your Home:

You may be experiencing VOC-related inflammation if you notice:
- Symptoms that improve when you're away from home for extended periods
- Headaches, brain fog, or fatigue that seem worse in certain rooms
- Respiratory symptoms or skin irritation without obvious allergic triggers
- "New building" or chemical odors that persist in your home
- Symptoms that worsen after cleaning, redecorating, or bringing new items into your home

Reducing VOC-Related Inflammatory Load:

➢ Immediate Actions:
- Increase ventilation by opening windows when outdoor air quality permits
- Remove synthetic air fresheners, plug-ins, and scented candles
- Switch to VOC-free or low-VOC cleaning products and personal care items

- Allow new furniture, carpets, and building materials to off-gas in garages or well-ventilated areas before bringing them into living spaces

➤ Long-term Strategies:
- Choose solid wood furniture over particle board or pressed wood products
- Select natural fiber carpets and rugs, or eliminate carpeting in favor of hard flooring
- Use natural materials like wool, cotton, and linen for bedding and window treatments
- Install activated carbon air purifiers in bedrooms and main living areas

Mold: The Hidden Inflammatory Amplifier

Mold exposure represents one of the most potent environmental inflammatory triggers. Even small amounts of mold can trigger significant inflammatory responses in sensitive individuals, and mold-related inflammation often persists long after exposure ends.

Mold produces mycotoxins—toxic compounds that trigger inflammatory cascades throughout your body. These toxins can accumulate in your tissues over time, creating chronic inflammatory states that resist traditional anti-inflammatory interventions.

Identifying Hidden Mold Exposure:

Look for these signs of potential mold issues in your home:
- Musty odors, particularly in basements, bathrooms, or areas with water damage
- Visible mold growth on walls, ceilings, or around windows
- Water stains or discoloration on walls or ceilings
- Condensation on windows or walls
- History of flooding, leaks, or water damage

➤ Health symptoms that may indicate mold-related inflammation:
- Respiratory symptoms that worsen at home
- Chronic fatigue that doesn't improve with rest
- Brain fog, memory problems, or difficulty concentrating
- Skin rashes or sensitivity that appears without other triggers
- Mood changes, anxiety, or depression that seems environmental

Addressing Mold-Related Inflammatory Triggers:

- Control humidity levels below 50% using dehumidifiers
- Ensure proper ventilation in bathrooms, kitchens, and laundry areas
- Address water leaks immediately and thoroughly dry affected areas
- Clean visible mold with hydrogen peroxide or other mold-specific cleaners
- Consider professional mold assessment if you suspect hidden mold problems
- Use HEPA air purifiers to remove mold spores from indoor air

Chemical Exposures in Personal Care and Household Products

The average person uses 9-15 personal care products daily, exposing themselves to over 100 unique chemicals before leaving the house. Many of these chemicals are known endocrine disruptors and inflammatory triggers that accumulate in your tissues over time.

Endocrine-Disrupting Chemicals (EDCs) and Inflammation

EDCs interfere with your body's hormonal systems, creating inflammatory responses throughout your endocrine network. These chemicals can mimic, block, or interfere with your natural hormones, leading to inflammatory cascades that affect metabolism, reproduction, mood, and immune function.

Common EDCs in household products include:
- Phthalates in fragranced products, plastics, and personal care items
- Parabens in cosmetics, lotions, and shampoos
- Triclosan in antibacterial soaps and toothpastes
- BPA and BPS in plastic containers and receipts
- Benzophenones in sunscreens and cosmetics

Creating a Low-Toxin Personal Care Routine:

➤ Morning Routine Modifications:
- Choose fragrance-free, organic personal care products
- Use natural deodorants without aluminum or synthetic fragrances
- Select mineral-based sunscreens with zinc oxide or titanium dioxide
- Avoid antibacterial soaps in favor of plain soap and water
- Choose organic makeup and cosmetics when possible

➤ Evening Routine Modifications:
- Use natural oils like jojoba or argan oil for moisturizing
- Choose toothpaste without triclosan, SLS, or artificial colors
- Select organic cotton or bamboo towels and washcloths
- Remove makeup with natural oils rather than chemical removers

Household Cleaning Product Transformation

Commercial cleaning products contain numerous inflammatory chemicals that create ongoing exposure through skin contact, inhalation, and residue on surfaces. Many of these chemicals are unnecessary for effective cleaning and can be replaced with safer alternatives.

➤ Building Your Non-Toxic Cleaning Arsenal:

- White vinegar for disinfecting and removing mineral deposits
- Baking soda for scrubbing and deodorizing
- Castile soap for general cleaning and dish washing
- Hydrogen peroxide for whitening and disinfecting
- Essential oils like tea tree, lavender, or lemon for natural antimicrobial action

Room-by-Room Cleaning Product Replacements:

➤ Kitchen:
- Dish soap: Castile soap with lemon essential oil
- Surface cleaner: White vinegar and water solution
- Oven cleaner: Baking soda paste with water
- Dish rinse aid: White vinegar

➤ Bathroom:
- Toilet cleaner: Baking soda and hydrogen peroxide
- Shower cleaner: White vinegar and dish soap mixture
- Mirror cleaner: Vinegar and water solution
- Mold remover: Hydrogen peroxide spray

➤ Laundry:
- Detergent: Fragrance-free, plant-based formulas
- Fabric softener: White vinegar or wool dryer balls
- Stain remover: Hydrogen peroxide or enzyme-based cleaners
- Bleach alternative: Oxygen bleach or hydrogen peroxide

Electromagnetic Field (EMF) Exposure and Inflammatory Response

Modern life surrounds you with electromagnetic fields from WiFi routers, cell phones, smart meters, and countless electronic devices. While the long-term health effects of EMF exposure continue to be studied, emerging research suggests that EMF exposure can trigger inflammatory responses in sensitive individuals.

EMF exposure may contribute to inflammation through several mechanisms:
- Disruption of cellular calcium channels, affecting cellular communication
- Interference with mitochondrial function and energy production
- Alteration of circadian rhythms through effects on melatonin production
- Activation of voltage-gated calcium channels, leading to oxidative stress

Identifying EMF Sensitivity and Inflammatory Responses

You may be experiencing EMF-related inflammatory responses if you notice:
- Symptoms that worsen in areas with high electronic device density
- Sleep disturbances that improve when devices are turned off or removed from the bedroom

- Headaches, brain fog, or fatigue that correlate with device usage
- Skin tingling or burning sensations near electronic devices
- Increased anxiety or irritability in electronically dense environments

Practical EMF Reduction Strategies

➢ Bedroom Optimization:
- Remove all electronic devices from the bedroom, including alarm clocks and charging stations
- Turn off WiFi routers at night or place them on timers
- Use battery-powered alarm clocks instead of phone alarms
- Consider EMF-blocking bed canopies for severely sensitive individuals
- Keep cell phones in airplane mode or in another room during sleep

➢ Daily EMF Management:
- Use speakerphone or wired headsets instead of holding phones to your head
- Maintain distance from WiFi routers and electronic devices when possible
- Take regular breaks from electronic devices throughout the day
- Spend time in nature away from electronic fields
- Consider hardwired internet connections instead of WiFi when feasible

➢ Home Environment Modifications:
- Replace wireless baby monitors with wired versions
- Use wired connections for computers and printers when possible
- Minimize the number of "smart" devices in your home
- Turn off devices when not in use rather than leaving them in standby mode
- Consider EMF meters to identify high-exposure areas in your home

Detoxification Support Through Targeted Nutrition

Your body possesses sophisticated detoxification systems designed to process and eliminate environmental toxins. However, the unprecedented toxic load of modern life often overwhelms these natural systems, leading to toxin accumulation and chronic inflammatory responses. Supporting your detoxification pathways through targeted nutrition can dramatically reduce your environmental inflammatory burden.

Your detoxification system operates primarily through your liver, kidneys, lungs, skin, and digestive system. This system works in two phases: Phase 1 detoxification transforms toxins into intermediate compounds, and Phase 2 detoxification converts these intermediates into water-soluble compounds that can be eliminated from your body.

Problems arise when Phase 1 and Phase 2 detoxification become imbalanced. If Phase 1 operates faster than Phase 2, toxic intermediate compounds accumulate, often causing more inflammatory damage than the original toxins. Supporting both phases simultaneously prevents this dangerous backup and ensures efficient toxin elimination.

Phase 1 Detoxification Support

Phase 1 detoxification relies on cytochrome P450 enzymes that require specific nutrients to function optimally. These enzymes transform fat-soluble toxins into intermediate compounds that can be processed by Phase 2 systems.

Key Phase 1 Supporting Nutrients:

➢ B-vitamins: Support enzyme cofactor functions and energy production for detoxification
 - Include: Leafy greens, nutritional yeast, organic liver, legumes
 - Focus: B2 (riboflavin), B3 (niacin), B6, B12, and folate

➢ Antioxidants: Protect cells from damage during the detoxification process
 - Include: Colorful berries, green tea, dark chocolate, turmeric
 - Focus: Vitamin C, vitamin E, selenium, and polyphenolic compounds

➢ Protein: Provides amino acids necessary for enzyme production
  - Include: High-quality animal proteins, hemp seeds, spirulina
  - Focus: Complete amino acid profiles with adequate methionine and cysteine

Phase 2 Detoxification Support

Phase 2 detoxification involves six major pathways that conjugate intermediate compounds with molecules that make them water-soluble and eliminable. Each pathway requires specific nutrients and can be supported through targeted dietary choices.

Glutathione Conjugation Pathway: This pathway handles many environmental toxins and requires adequate glutathione production.

- Supporting foods: Cruciferous vegetables, garlic, onions, eggs
- Key nutrients: N-acetylcysteine, glycine, glutamine
- Preparation tips: Lightly steam broccoli and cauliflower to preserve sulforaphane content

Sulfation Pathway: This pathway processes hormones, food additives, and environmental chemicals.

- Supporting foods: Eggs, fish, garlic, onions, cruciferous vegetables
- Key nutrients: Sulfur-containing amino acids, molybdenum
- Preparation tips: Include raw garlic and onions daily for maximum sulfur compounds

Glucuronidation Pathway: This pathway eliminates hormones, medications, and environmental toxins.

- Supporting foods: Cruciferous vegetables, citrus fruits, berries
- Key nutrients: Glucuronic acid, vitamin C, magnesium
- Preparation tips: Include citrus peels in smoothies or teas for limonene content

Methylation Pathway: This pathway processes hormones, heavy metals, and histamine.

- Supporting foods: Leafy greens, legumes, beets, organic liver
- Key nutrients: Folate, B12, choline, betaine
- Preparation tips: Steam or sauté leafy greens to improve folate availability

Acetylation Pathway: This pathway handles environmental chemicals and some medications.

- Supporting foods: Garlic, onions, cruciferous vegetables
- Key nutrients: Acetyl-CoA, pantothenic acid
- Preparation tips: Crush garlic and let sit 10 minutes before cooking to activate beneficial compounds

Amino Acid Conjugation Pathway: This pathway processes benzoic acid and other environmental chemicals.

- Supporting foods: High-quality proteins, bone broth, collagen
- Key nutrients: Glycine, taurine, glutamine
- Preparation tips: Include bone broth regularly for glycine and other amino acids

Targeted Nutritional Protocols for Environmental Detoxification

Different environmental exposures require specific nutritional support strategies. By identifying your primary exposures, you can tailor your detoxification support for maximum effectiveness.

Heavy Metal Detoxification Support

Heavy metals like lead, mercury, cadmium, and aluminum accumulate in tissues over time, creating ongoing inflammatory stress. These metals interfere with enzyme function and generate oxidative stress throughout your body.

➢ Chelation-Supporting Foods:
- Cilantro: Contains compounds that bind to heavy metals and support elimination
- Chlorella: Binds to heavy metals in the digestive tract and prevents reabsorption
- Garlic: Provides sulfur compounds that support heavy metal elimination

- Brazil nuts: Provide selenium, which protects against mercury toxicity
- Parsley: Contains compounds that support kidney detoxification of metals

➢ Heavy Metal Detox Protocol:
- Morning: Chlorella (3-5 grams) with lemon water
- Meals: Include cilantro and parsley in salads and smoothies
- Evening: Brazil nuts (2-3 nuts) for selenium support
- Weekly: Epsom salt baths to support transdermal detoxification

Chemical Detoxification Support

Petrochemicals, pesticides, and industrial chemicals require robust Phase 1 and Phase 2 detoxification support. These chemicals often accumulate in fatty tissues and require specific nutrients to mobilize and eliminate safely.

➢ Chemical Detox Supporting Foods:
- Cruciferous vegetables: Provide indole-3-carbinol and sulforaphane for enzyme induction
- Green tea: Provides EGCG and other polyphenols that support detoxification
- Turmeric: Enhances both Phase 1 and Phase 2 detoxification pathways
- Milk thistle: Protects liver cells during detoxification processes
- Burdock root: Supports lymphatic drainage and liver function

➢ Chemical Detox Protocol:
- Daily: 2-3 cups green tea between meals
- Meals: Include cruciferous vegetables at least twice daily
- Seasoning: Use turmeric with black pepper in cooking
- Weekly: Dry brushing before showers to support lymphatic drainage

Mold Mycotoxin Detoxification Support

Mycotoxins from mold exposure require specialized detoxification support because these toxins can persist in tissues long after exposure ends. Mycotoxins often interfere with mitochondrial function and require specific nutrients to eliminate safely.

➢ Mycotoxin Detox Supporting Foods:
- Activated charcoal: Binds mycotoxins in the digestive tract (take away from other supplements)
- Bentonite clay: Provides additional binding capacity for mycotoxins
- Pomegranate: Contains compounds that support cellular repair from mycotoxin damage
- Green leafy vegetables: Provide chlorophyll, which supports detoxification
- Coconut oil: Provides medium-chain fatty acids that support mitochondrial function

➢ Mycotoxin Detox Protocol:
- Morning: Activated charcoal (1-2 grams) away from food and supplements
- Meals: Include bitter greens like arugula and dandelion
- Snacks: Pomegranate seeds or fresh pomegranate juice
- Evening: Bentonite clay (1 teaspoon in water) before bed

Chemical Exposures and Protective Nutritional Strategies

Beyond supporting your body's natural detoxification systems, specific nutrients can provide direct protection against chemical exposures, reducing the inflammatory damage these chemicals cause and supporting your body's resilience against ongoing exposures.

Antioxidant Protection Against Chemical Damage

Chemical exposures generate free radicals and oxidative stress that trigger inflammatory cascades throughout your body. Strategic antioxidant intake can neutralize these free radicals before they cause cellular damage, preventing the inflammatory responses that follow chemical exposure.

The Antioxidant Network Approach

Rather than relying on single antioxidants, the most effective protection comes from consuming antioxidants that work together in networks. These antioxidant networks regenerate each other, providing sustained protection against chemical-induced oxidative stress.

➤ Primary Antioxidant Network:
- Vitamin C: Water-soluble antioxidant that protects cellular fluids
- Vitamin E: Fat-soluble antioxidant that protects cell membranes
- Glutathione: Master antioxidant that regenerates other antioxidants
- Alpha-lipoic acid: Antioxidant that works in both water and fat-soluble environments

➤ Supporting Antioxidant Network:
- Coenzyme Q10: Protects mitochondria from chemical damage
- N-acetylcysteine: Precursor to glutathione production
- Selenium: Cofactor for glutathione peroxidase enzyme
- Zinc: Cofactor for superoxide dismutase enzyme

Food-Based Antioxidant Strategies

➤ High-ORAC (Oxygen Radical Absorbance Capacity) Foods: Include these foods daily to maximize antioxidant protection:
- Berries: Blueberries, blackberries, goji berries, acai
- Herbs and spices: Oregano, turmeric, cinnamon, cloves
- Dark chocolate: 70% cacao or higher
- Green tea: 3-4 cups daily for maximum polyphenol content
- Colorful vegetables: Purple cabbage, beets, carrots, bell peppers

➤ Antioxidant Timing Strategies:
- Pre-exposure: Consume high-antioxidant foods before known chemical exposures
- During exposure: Carry antioxidant-rich snacks for ongoing protection
- Post-exposure: Include extra antioxidants to support recovery and repair

Specific Protective Strategies for Common Chemical Exposures

Different chemicals require specific protective approaches based on their mechanisms of toxicity and routes of exposure. Understanding these specific protections allows you to tailor your nutritional defense against your most common exposures.

Pesticide Exposure Protection

Pesticides work by disrupting nervous system function in insects, but they can also affect human neurological function and trigger inflammatory responses.

➤ Pesticide Protection Protocol:
- Acetylcholine support: Include eggs, fish, and lecithin to support neurotransmitter production
- Liver support: Consume milk thistle tea and dandelion greens to enhance pesticide metabolism
- Nervous system protection: Include omega-3 fatty acids and B-vitamins
- Immediate protection: Wash all produce thoroughly and choose organic for the "Dirty Dozen" fruits and vegetables

Air Pollution Protection

Air pollution contains multiple inflammatory compounds that affect respiratory and cardiovascular systems.

➤ Air Pollution Protection Protocol:
- Respiratory support: Include anti-inflammatory foods like ginger, turmeric, and garlic
- Cardiovascular protection: Focus on omega-3 fatty acids and magnesium-rich foods
- Detoxification support: Include cruciferous vegetables and green tea
- Immediate protection: Use HEPA air purifiers indoors and avoid outdoor exercise during high pollution periods

Plastic Chemical Protection

Plastics contain endocrine-disrupting chemicals that accumulate in fatty tissues and interfere with hormonal function.

➤ Plastic Chemical Protection Protocol:*
- Hormone support: Include cruciferous vegetables to support healthy hormone metabolism

- Liver support: Consume foods that enhance Phase 2 detoxification
- Fat tissue protection: Include antioxidants that concentrate in fatty tissues
- Immediate protection: Minimize plastic food containers and choose glass or stainless steel alternatives

Creating Your Personal Environmental Protection Plan

Your environmental protection plan should address your specific exposures while supporting your body's natural resilience against chemical stress. This personalized approach ensures that you're focusing your efforts on the interventions that will provide the greatest benefit for your situation.

Environmental Exposure Assessment

➢ High-Risk Environments:
- Urban areas with significant air pollution
- Agricultural regions with pesticide exposure
- Industrial areas with chemical emissions
- New buildings with off-gassing materials
- Homes with mold or water damage issues

➢ Occupational Exposures:
- Healthcare workers exposed to chemicals and pharmaceuticals
- Agricultural workers with pesticide exposure
- Manufacturing workers with industrial chemical exposure
- Hairdressers and nail technicians with cosmetic chemical exposure
- Cleaning professionals with chemical cleaner exposure

➢ Lifestyle Exposures:
- Frequent air travel with increased radiation and chemical exposure
- Regular use of personal care products with synthetic ingredients
- Living in homes with synthetic materials and furnishings
- Frequent consumption of processed foods with additives
- Use of conventional cleaning and lawn care products

Prioritized Protection Strategies

Based on your exposure assessment, prioritize your protection strategies:

➢ Tier 1 - Essential Protections (Implement Immediately):
- Remove the most toxic exposures from your immediate environment
- Support basic detoxification with daily cruciferous vegetables and green tea
- Ensure adequate antioxidant intake through colorful fruits and vegetables
- Optimize sleep and stress management to support natural detoxification

➢ Tier 2 - Enhanced Protections (Implement Within 30 Days):
- Address specific exposures with targeted nutritional protocols
- Upgrade personal care and household products to non-toxic alternatives
- Install air and water filtration systems as budget allows
- Add specific detoxification supporting foods to your daily routine

➢ Tier 3 - Advanced Protections (Implement Within 90 Days):
- Consider targeted supplementation for specific exposures
- Implement regular detoxification protocols like sauna therapy
- Address underlying health issues that impair detoxification
- Create low-toxin zones in your home for recovery and restoration

Your environmental protection plan should be sustainable and adaptable to changing circumstances. Focus on the strategies that provide the greatest impact with the least disruption to your lifestyle, gradually building toward more comprehensive protection as you develop new habits and resources.

Remember that environmental factors represent just one component of your total inflammatory load. The most effective approach combines environmental protection with the dietary, lifestyle, and stress management strategies outlined in other chapters, creating a comprehensive anti-inflammatory lifestyle that addresses all sources of chronic inflammation in your life.

Therapeutic Smoothies and Elixirs

Golden Turmeric Smoothie

Prep Time: 5 minutes Chill Time: 15 minutes Serves: 2

1 cup unsweetened coconut milk

1/2 cup frozen mango chunks

1/2 frozen banana

1 tablespoon fresh turmeric root, grated (or 1 teaspoon ground turmeric)

1 teaspoon fresh ginger root, grated

1/4 teaspoon black pepper

1 tablespoon coconut oil

1 tablespoon raw honey

1/2 cup ice cubes

Pinch of sea salt

Combine coconut milk, mango, banana, turmeric, ginger, black pepper, coconut oil, and honey in high-speed blender. Blend on high speed for 60 seconds until completely smooth and creamy. Add ice cubes and blend additional 30 seconds until frothy. Add sea salt and pulse twice to incorporate. Pour into chilled glasses and serve immediately. For enhanced absorption, consume with a small amount of healthy fat such as coconut oil or avocado.

GREEN POWERHOUSE

Prep Time: 8 minutes Chill Time: 10 minutes Serves: 2

1 cup filtered water

1/2 cup coconut water

2 cups fresh spinach leaves

1/2 cucumber, peeled and chopped

1/2 avocado, pitted and peeled

1 tablespoon fresh parsley

1 tablespoon fresh cilantro

1 inch fresh ginger root, peeled

Juice of 1 lemon

1 tablespoon hemp seeds

1/2 teaspoon spirulina powder

1/4 teaspoon sea salt

Add filtered water and coconut water to blender first to ensure proper blending. Layer spinach, cucumber, avocado, parsley, cilantro, and ginger into blender. Blend on medium speed for 45 seconds until vegetables are fully broken down. Add lemon juice, hemp seeds, spirulina, and sea salt. Blend on high speed for additional 30 seconds until smooth and vibrant green. Strain through fine mesh if desired for smoother texture. Serve immediately over ice for optimal nutrient retention.

Tart Cherry Anti-Pain Elixir

Prep Time: 10 minutes Steeping Time: 5 minutes Serves: 2

1 cup pure tart cherry juice (unsweetened)

1/2 cup chamomile tea, cooled

1 tablespoon fresh lemon juice

1 tablespoon raw apple cider vinegar

1 teaspoon raw honey

1/2 teaspoon ground cinnamon

1/4 teaspoon ground ginger

Pinch of cayenne pepper

1/2 cup sparkling water

Fresh mint leaves for garnish

Brew chamomile tea using 1 cup hot water and 2 tea bags. Steep for 5 minutes, then remove bags and allow to cool completely. In mixing bowl, whisk together tart cherry juice, cooled chamomile tea, lemon juice, apple cider vinegar, and honey until honey dissolves completely. Add cinnamon, ginger, and cayenne pepper. Whisk thoroughly to combine all spices. Strain mixture through fine mesh strainer to remove any spice particles. Add sparkling water just before serving. Pour over ice and garnish with fresh mint leaves. Consume 30 minutes before bedtime for optimal anti-inflammatory and sleep benefits.

OMEGA-3 BRAIN BOOST SMOOTHIE

Prep Time: 7 minutes Chill Time: 20 minutes Serves: 2

1 cup unsweetened almond milk

1/2 cup fresh or frozen blueberries

1/2 cup fresh or frozen blackberries

1/4 cup walnuts, soaked for 2 hours

2 tablespoons ground flaxseeds

1 tablespoon chia seeds

1 tablespoon almond butter

1 teaspoon vanilla extract

1/2 teaspoon ground cinnamon

1 tablespoon raw honey

1/2 cup ice cubes

Soak walnuts in filtered water for 2 hours before preparation to improve digestibility and nutrient absorption. Drain and rinse soaked walnuts thoroughly. Combine almond milk, blueberries, blackberries, soaked walnuts, ground flaxseeds, chia seeds, and almond butter in high-speed blender. Blend on high speed for 90 seconds until completely smooth and creamy. Add vanilla extract, cinnamon, and honey. Blend additional 30 seconds to incorporate. Add ice cubes and blend until frothy and well-chilled. Allow to sit for 2 minutes to let chia seeds expand slightly. Stir before serving to distribute seeds evenly. Consume within 30 minutes for optimal omega-3 stability.

GINGER DIGESTIVE FIRE ELIXIR

Prep Time: 15 minutes Cooking Time: 10 minutes Serves: 3

2 cups filtered water

2 inches fresh ginger root, sliced thin

1 tablespoon fresh turmeric root, sliced (or 1 teaspoon ground)

1 cinnamon stick

4 whole cloves

1 star anise pod

1 tablespoon raw honey

2 tablespoons fresh lemon juice

1/4 teaspoon black pepper

Pinch of sea salt

1 tablespoon coconut oil

Bring filtered water to gentle boil in small saucepan. Add sliced ginger, turmeric, cinnamon stick, cloves, and star anise. Reduce heat to low simmer and cover. Simmer for 10 minutes to extract maximum therapeutic compounds. Remove from heat and allow to steep additional 5 minutes. Strain liquid through fine mesh strainer, pressing solids to extract maximum flavor. Discard solids. While liquid is still warm, whisk in honey until completely dissolved. Add lemon juice, black pepper, and sea salt. Whisk in coconut oil until emulsified. Serve warm in small cups. Consume 20 minutes before meals to stimulate digestive fire and reduce inflammation. Store refrigerated for up to 3 days and reheat gently before serving.

ADAPTOGENIC STRESS-RELIEF SMOOTHIE

Prep Time: 6 minutes Chill Time: 15 minutes Serves: 2

1 cup coconut milk (full-fat)

1/2 cup cashews, soaked for 1 hour

1 frozen banana

1 tablespoon cacao powder

1 teaspoon ashwagandha powder

1/2 teaspoon reishi mushroom powder

1/2 teaspoon maca powder

1 tablespoon coconut butter

1 tablespoon raw honey

1 teaspoon vanilla extract

1/4 teaspoon sea salt

1/2 cup ice cubes

Soak cashews in filtered water for 1 hour to soften. Drain and rinse thoroughly. Combine coconut milk, soaked cashews, and frozen banana in high-speed blender. Blend on high speed for 60 seconds until completely smooth and creamy. Add cacao powder, ashwagandha, reishi, maca, coconut butter, honey, vanilla, and sea salt. Blend on high speed for additional 45 seconds until all powders are fully incorporated and mixture is smooth. Add ice cubes and blend until frothy and well-chilled. Taste and adjust sweetness if needed. Pour into chilled glasses and consume immediately. For best results, consume in afternoon to support stress resilience without interfering with sleep.

Beet Liver Detox Elixir

Prep Time: 12 minutes Chill Time: 30 minutes Serves: 2

1 medium raw beet, peeled and chopped

1 cup filtered water

1/2 cup fresh carrot juice

1/4 cup fresh lemon juice

1 tablespoon fresh ginger root, grated

1 clove garlic, minced

1 tablespoon raw apple cider vinegar

1 teaspoon raw honey

1/4 teaspoon ground cardamom

1/4 teaspoon ground fennel

Pinch of sea salt

Fresh mint leaves for garnish

Peel and chop beet into small pieces to facilitate blending. Combine chopped beet with filtered water in high-speed blender. Blend on high speed for 90 seconds until beet is completely liquefied. Strain through fine mesh strainer or cheesecloth, pressing solids to extract maximum juice. Reserve 3/4 cup of beet juice and discard pulp. In clean blender, combine beet juice, carrot juice, lemon juice, grated ginger, and minced garlic. Blend on medium speed for 30 seconds until well combined. Add apple cider vinegar, honey, cardamom, fennel, and sea salt. Blend additional 15 seconds until spices are incorporated. Chill in refrigerator for 30 minutes before serving. Strain again if desired for smoother texture. Serve over ice and garnish with fresh mint. Consume on empty stomach in morning for optimal detoxification support.

COLLAGEN REPAIR SMOOTHIE

Prep Time: 5 minutes Chill Time: 10 minutes Serves: 2

1 cup bone broth, cooled

1/2 cup coconut milk

1/2 cup frozen pineapple chunks

1/4 cup fresh spinach leaves

2 tablespoons grass-fed collagen peptides

1 tablespoon coconut oil

1 teaspoon raw honey

1/2 teaspoon vanilla extract

1/4 teaspoon ground ginger

Juice of 1/2 lime

1/2 cup ice cubes

Ensure bone broth is completely cooled before blending to prevent collagen from clumping. Combine cooled bone broth, coconut milk, frozen pineapple, and spinach in high-speed blender. Blend on medium speed for 45 seconds until spinach is completely broken down. Add collagen peptides gradually while blender is running on low speed to prevent clumping. Increase to high speed and blend for 30 seconds until collagen is fully dissolved. Add coconut oil, honey, vanilla, ginger, and lime juice. Blend additional 30 seconds until smooth and creamy. Add ice cubes and blend until frothy and well-chilled. Serve immediately to preserve collagen integrity. Consume post-workout or in evening to support tissue repair and recovery.

HIBISCUS ANTIOXIDANT ELIXIR

Prep Time: 8 minutes Steeping Time: 15 minutes Serves: 2

2 cups filtered water

2 tablespoons dried hibiscus flowers

1 cup fresh or frozen mixed berries

1 tablespoon raw honey

1 tablespoon fresh lime juice

1/2 teaspoon ground cinnamon

1/4 teaspoon ground cardamom

Pinch of black pepper

1 tablespoon coconut oil

Fresh berries for garnish

Bring filtered water to boil in small saucepan. Remove from heat and add dried hibiscus flowers. Cover and steep for 15 minutes to extract maximum antioxidants. Strain through fine mesh strainer, pressing flowers to extract liquid. Discard spent flowers. Allow hibiscus tea to cool to room temperature. In high-speed blender, combine cooled hibiscus tea and mixed berries. Blend on high speed for 60 seconds until berries are completely pureed. Strain through fine mesh strainer if smooth texture is desired, or leave unstrained for additional fiber. Add honey, lime juice, cinnamon, cardamom, and black pepper. Whisk thoroughly until honey dissolves completely. Gradually whisk in coconut oil until emulsified. Chill in refrigerator until cold. Serve over ice and garnish with fresh berries. Consume between meals for optimal antioxidant absorption.

MATCHA GREEN TEA RECOVERY SMOOTHIE

Prep Time: 6 minutes Chill Time: 10 minutes Serves: 2

1 cup unsweetened almond milk

1/2 cup coconut water

1/2 frozen banana

1/4 cup fresh spinach leaves

1 tablespoon ceremonial grade matcha powder

1 tablespoon coconut butter

1 tablespoon raw honey

1 teaspoon vanilla extract

1/4 teaspoon ground ginger

Pinch of sea salt

1/2 cup ice cubes

Coconut flakes for garnish

Sift matcha powder through fine mesh strainer to remove any lumps before adding to blender. Combine almond milk, coconut water, frozen banana, and spinach in high-speed blender. Blend on medium speed for 45 seconds until spinach is completely incorporated. Add sifted matcha powder gradually while blender runs on low speed to prevent clumping. Increase to high speed and blend for 30 seconds until matcha is fully dissolved and mixture is bright green. Add coconut butter, honey, vanilla, ginger, and sea salt. Blend additional 30 seconds until smooth and creamy. Add ice cubes and blend until frothy and well-chilled. Pour into chilled glasses and garnish with coconut flakes. Consume in morning or early afternoon to avoid caffeine interference with sleep. Serve immediately to preserve matcha's antioxidant potency.

Breakfast Bowls and Options

GOLDEN TURMERIC QUINOA POWER BOWL

Prep Time: 15 minutes Cook Time: 20 minutes Serves: 2

1 cup tri-color quinoa, rinsed thoroughly

2 cups unsweetened coconut milk

1 tablespoon fresh turmeric root, grated

1 teaspoon ground cinnamon

1/4 teaspoon ground ginger

1/4 teaspoon black pepper

2 tablespoons raw honey

1/4 cup chopped walnuts

1/4 cup hemp seeds

1/2 cup fresh blueberries

1 tablespoon coconut flakes

Pinch of sea salt

Combine rinsed quinoa with coconut milk in medium saucepan over medium heat. Add grated turmeric, cinnamon, ginger, black pepper, and sea salt. Bring mixture to gentle boil, then reduce heat to low and cover. Simmer for 18-20 minutes until quinoa is tender and liquid is absorbed. Remove from heat and allow to rest for 5 minutes. Fluff quinoa with fork and drizzle with honey while still warm. Divide between two bowls and top with chopped walnuts, hemp seeds, fresh blueberries, and coconut flakes. Serve immediately while warm for optimal nutrient absorption and anti-inflammatory benefits.

OMEGA-3 CHIA SEED PUDDING BOWL

Prep Time: 10 minutes Chill Time: 4 hours Serves: 2

1/4 cup chia seeds

1 cup unsweetened almond milk

2 tablespoons ground flaxseeds

1 tablespoon almond butter

1 tablespoon raw honey

1 teaspoon vanilla extract

1/2 teaspoon ground cinnamon

1/4 cup fresh raspberries

1/4 cup fresh blackberries

2 tablespoons chopped almonds

1 tablespoon cacao nibs

Fresh mint leaves for garnish

Whisk together chia seeds, almond milk, ground flaxseeds, almond butter, honey, vanilla extract, and cinnamon in mixing bowl until completely smooth. Ensure chia seeds are evenly distributed to prevent clumping. Cover bowl and refrigerate for minimum 4 hours or overnight, stirring once after first hour to redistribute seeds. When ready to serve, divide pudding between two bowls. Top with fresh raspberries, blackberries, chopped almonds, and cacao nibs. Garnish with fresh mint leaves. The pudding will keep refrigerated for up to three days, making it ideal for meal preparation.

GREEN GODDESS AVOCADO BOWL

Prep Time: 12 minutes Serves: 2

2 ripe avocados, halved and pitted

1 cup fresh spinach leaves, chopped

1/4 cup fresh cilantro, chopped

1/4 cup fresh parsley, chopped

2 tablespoons hemp seeds

2 tablespoons pumpkin seeds

1 tablespoon extra virgin olive oil

1 tablespoon fresh lemon juice

1 tablespoon nutritional yeast

1/2 teaspoon garlic powder

1/4 teaspoon sea salt

1/4 teaspoon black pepper

2 soft-boiled eggs

Cherry tomatoes for garnish

Scoop avocado flesh into mixing bowl, leaving shells intact for serving if desired. Mash avocados to desired consistency, leaving some texture for optimal satisfaction. Add chopped spinach, cilantro, parsley, hemp seeds, and pumpkin seeds to mashed avocado. Drizzle with olive oil and lemon juice, then sprinkle with nutritional yeast, garlic powder, sea salt, and black pepper. Mix gently to combine all ingredients while maintaining texture. Prepare soft-boiled eggs by boiling for exactly 6 minutes, then immediately transferring to ice bath. Divide avocado mixture between two bowls and top each with one soft-boiled egg. Garnish with cherry tomatoes and serve immediately.

BERRY YOGURT BOWL

Prep Time: 8 minutes Serves: 2

1 cup plain Greek yogurt, full-fat

2 tablespoons raw honey

1 teaspoon vanilla extract

1/2 cup fresh strawberries, sliced

1/2 cup fresh blueberries

1/4 cup fresh raspberries

2 tablespoons ground flaxseeds

2 tablespoons chia seeds

1/4 cup chopped pecans

1 tablespoon bee pollen

1/2 teaspoon ground cinnamon

Fresh basil leaves for garnish

Combine Greek yogurt, honey, and vanilla extract in mixing bowl, whisking until smooth and creamy. Divide yogurt mixture between two serving bowls, creating smooth base layer. Arrange fresh strawberries, blueberries, and raspberries in colorful sections over yogurt. Sprinkle ground flaxseeds and chia seeds evenly across berries for omega-3 enhancement. Add chopped pecans for healthy fats and satisfying texture. Dust with ground cinnamon and finish with bee pollen for additional anti-inflammatory compounds. Garnish with fresh basil leaves for aromatic enhancement. Serve immediately to preserve probiotic benefits and fresh fruit quality.

WARMING GINGER OAT BOWL

Prep Time: 5 minutes Cook Time: 15 minutes Serves: 2

1 cup steel-cut oats

2 cups filtered water

1 cup unsweetened coconut milk

2 tablespoons fresh ginger root, grated

1 teaspoon ground cinnamon

1/2 teaspoon ground cardamom

1/4 teaspoon ground cloves

2 tablespoons raw honey

1/4 cup chopped walnuts

2 tablespoons dried goji berries

1 tablespoon coconut oil

Pinch of sea salt

Bring filtered water to boil in medium saucepan, then add steel-cut oats and sea salt. Reduce heat to medium-low and simmer uncovered for 10 minutes, stirring occasionally. Add coconut milk, grated ginger, cinnamon, cardamom, and cloves to oats. Continue cooking for additional 5-8 minutes until oats reach desired consistency and spices are well incorporated. Remove from heat and stir in honey and coconut oil until melted and distributed. Divide between two bowls and top with chopped walnuts and goji berries. Allow to cool slightly before serving to prevent burning. The warming spices will continue to develop flavor as the bowl cools to eating temperature.

PROTEIN-PACKED QUINOA BREAKFAST BOWL

Prep Time: 10 minutes Cook Time: 25 minutes Serves: 2

3/4 cup quinoa, rinsed

1 1/2 cups vegetable broth

2 large eggs

1 cup fresh spinach leaves

1/2 cup cherry tomatoes, halved

1/4 cup red onion, diced

2 tablespoons extra virgin olive oil

1 tablespoon apple cider vinegar

1 tablespoon fresh lemon juice

2 tablespoons sunflower seeds

2 tablespoons fresh dill, chopped

1/2 teaspoon garlic powder

Sea salt and black pepper to taste

Cook quinoa by combining with vegetable broth in saucepan, bringing to boil, then reducing heat and simmering covered for 15 minutes until tender. Remove from heat and fluff with fork. Meanwhile, prepare soft-boiled eggs by boiling for 7 minutes, then transferring to ice bath and peeling when cool. Sauté spinach in 1 tablespoon olive oil until just wilted, seasoning with salt and pepper. Combine cherry tomatoes and red onion in small bowl. Whisk together remaining olive oil, apple cider vinegar, lemon juice, and garlic powder for dressing. Divide warm quinoa between bowls, top with sautéed spinach, tomato mixture, and halved soft-boiled eggs. Drizzle with dressing, sprinkle with sunflower seeds and fresh dill before serving.

MEDITERRANEAN HERB BOWL

Prep Time: 15 minutes Cook Time: 10 minutes Serves: 2

1 cup pearl couscous (Israeli couscous)

2 cups low-sodium chicken broth

1/4 cup extra virgin olive oil

2 tablespoons fresh lemon juice

1/4 cup fresh oregano, chopped

1/4 cup fresh basil, chopped

2 tablespoons fresh mint, chopped

1/2 cup kalamata olives, pitted and halved

1/2 cup cherry tomatoes, quartered

1/4 cup pine nuts, toasted

2 tablespoons capers, drained

1/4 cup feta cheese, crumbled

Sea salt and black pepper to taste

Cook pearl couscous according to package directions using chicken broth instead of water for enhanced flavor. Drain and transfer to large mixing bowl. While couscous is still warm, drizzle with olive oil and lemon juice, tossing to coat evenly. Add fresh oregano, basil, and mint, stirring gently to distribute herbs throughout. Fold in kalamata olives, cherry tomatoes, toasted pine nuts, and capers. Season with sea salt and black pepper to taste, keeping in mind that olives and capers provide natural saltiness. Divide between serving bowls and top with crumbled feta cheese. Serve warm or at room temperature. This bowl can be prepared ahead and refrigerated, though herbs are best added just before serving.

COCONUT CURRY BREAKFAST BOWL

Prep Time: 8 minutes Cook Time: 20 minutes Serves: 2

1 cup brown rice, cooked and cooled

1 can full-fat coconut milk

1 tablespoon yellow curry powder

1 tablespoon fresh turmeric root, grated

1 teaspoon fresh ginger root, grated

1 clove garlic, minced

1 tablespoon coconut oil

1 cup baby spinach leaves

1/2 red bell pepper, diced

1/4 cup cashews, chopped

2 tablespoons fresh cilantro, chopped

1 tablespoon lime juice

Sea salt to taste

Heat coconut oil in large skillet over medium heat. Add curry powder and cook for 30 seconds until fragrant. Add grated turmeric, ginger, and minced garlic, cooking for additional 30 seconds while stirring constantly. Pour in coconut milk and bring to gentle simmer. Add cooked brown rice to skillet, stirring to coat with curry mixture. Simmer for 5 minutes until rice absorbs some liquid and flavors meld. Add baby spinach and red bell pepper, cooking until spinach wilts and pepper softens slightly. Remove from heat and stir in lime juice and sea salt to taste. Divide between bowls and top with chopped cashews and fresh cilantro. Serve immediately while warm for optimal flavor and texture.

ANTIOXIDANT ACAI BOWL

Prep Time: 10 minutes Serves: 2

2 frozen acai packets, thawed slightly

1/2 frozen banana

1/4 cup coconut water

1 tablespoon almond butter

1 tablespoon raw honey

1/4 cup fresh strawberries, sliced

1/4 cup fresh blueberries

2 tablespoons granola (grain-free preferred)

2 tablespoons coconut flakes

1 tablespoon chia seeds

1 tablespoon cacao nibs

Fresh mint leaves for garnish

Break up thawed acai packets and combine with frozen banana, coconut water, almond butter, and honey in high-speed blender. Blend on high speed until mixture reaches thick, smooth consistency similar to soft-serve ice cream. Add small amounts of coconut water if needed, but keep mixture thick enough to support toppings. Divide acai mixture between two bowls, smoothing tops with spoon. Arrange fresh strawberries and blueberries in decorative pattern over acai base. Sprinkle with granola, coconut flakes, chia seeds, and cacao nibs. Garnish with fresh mint leaves for aromatic finish. Serve immediately before mixture softens.

SAVORY MUSHROOM AND HERB BOWL

Prep Time: 12 minutes Cook Time: 15 minutes Serves: 2

2 cups mixed mushrooms, sliced (shiitake, cremini, oyster)

2 tablespoons extra virgin olive oil

2 cloves garlic, minced

1 tablespoon fresh thyme leaves

1 tablespoon fresh rosemary, chopped

1 cup cooked farro

2 large eggs

2 cups arugula

1/4 cup goat cheese, crumbled

2 tablespoons balsamic vinegar

1 tablespoon raw honey

Sea salt and black pepper to taste

Heat olive oil in large skillet over medium-high heat. Add sliced mushrooms and cook without stirring for 3-4 minutes until golden brown on one side. Stir and continue cooking for 2-3 minutes until mushrooms are tender and caramelized. Add minced garlic, thyme, and rosemary, cooking for additional minute until fragrant. Season with sea salt and black pepper. In small bowl, whisk together balsamic vinegar and honey to create glaze. In separate pan, fry eggs to desired doneness. Divide cooked farro between bowls and top with sautéed mushroom mixture. Add fresh arugula and crumbled goat cheese. Top each bowl with fried egg and drizzle with balsamic honey glaze. Serve immediately while eggs are warm.

WARMING SWEET POTATO HASH BOWL

Prep Time: 10 minutes Cook Time: 25 minutes Serves: 2

2 medium sweet potatoes, diced small

1 red bell pepper, diced

1 small red onion, diced

2 tablespoons coconut oil

1 teaspoon ground cumin

1/2 teaspoon smoked paprika

1/4 teaspoon cayenne pepper

2 large eggs

1/4 cup fresh cilantro, chopped

2 tablespoons pumpkin seeds

1 avocado, sliced

Lime wedges for serving

Sea salt and black pepper to taste

Preheat oven to 425 degrees Fahrenheit. Toss diced sweet potatoes with 1 tablespoon coconut oil, cumin, smoked paprika, cayenne pepper, sea salt, and black pepper. Spread on baking sheet and roast for 15 minutes. Add diced bell pepper and red onion to baking sheet, tossing with remaining coconut oil. Continue roasting for 8-10 minutes until sweet potatoes are tender and vegetables are lightly caramelized. Meanwhile, prepare eggs to desired doneness in separate skillet. Divide roasted vegetable hash between bowls and top with cooked eggs. Garnish with fresh cilantro, pumpkin seeds, and avocado slices. Serve with lime wedges for additional flavor enhancement.

Protein-Rich Lentil Bowl

Prep Time: 5 minutes Cook Time: 30 minutes Serves: 2

1 cup red lentils, rinsed

2 cups vegetable broth

1 tablespoon coconut oil

1 small onion, diced

2 cloves garlic, minced

1 tablespoon fresh ginger, grated

1 teaspoon ground turmeric

1/2 teaspoon ground coriander

1 cup baby spinach

1/4 cup fresh parsley, chopped

2 tablespoons tahini

1 tablespoon lemon juice

2 tablespoons hemp seeds

Sea salt and black pepper to taste

Cook red lentils by combining with vegetable broth in saucepan, bringing to boil, then simmering covered for 15-20 minutes until tender. Meanwhile, heat coconut oil in large skillet over medium heat. Add diced onion and cook for 5 minutes until softened. Add minced garlic, grated ginger, turmeric, and coriander, cooking for additional minute until fragrant. Add cooked lentils to skillet with aromatics, stirring to combine. Add baby spinach and cook until wilted. Remove from heat and stir in fresh parsley. In small bowl, whisk together tahini and lemon juice until smooth. Divide lentil mixture between bowls, drizzle with tahini dressing, and sprinkle with hemp seeds. Season with sea salt and black pepper before serving.

Spiced Apple Cinnamon Bowl

Prep Time: 8 minutes Cook Time: 12 minutes Serves: 2

2 large apples, peeled and diced

2 tablespoons coconut oil

1 tablespoon raw honey

1 teaspoon ground cinnamon

1/4 teaspoon ground nutmeg

1/4 teaspoon ground ginger

1 cup rolled oats, cooked

1/4 cup pecans, chopped

2 tablespoons ground flaxseeds

1/4 cup unsweetened almond milk

1 tablespoon almond butter

Pinch of sea salt

Heat coconut oil in large skillet over medium heat. Add diced apples and cook for 5-6 minutes until beginning to soften. Add honey, cinnamon, nutmeg, ginger, and sea salt, stirring to coat apples evenly. Continue cooking for 3-4 minutes until apples are tender and caramelized. Meanwhile, prepare oats according to package directions, using water or plant milk. In small bowl, whisk together almond milk and almond butter until smooth. Divide cooked oats between bowls and top with spiced apple mixture. Sprinkle with chopped pecans and ground flaxseeds. Drizzle with almond butter mixture before serving. The warming spices provide anti-inflammatory benefits while creating comforting autumn flavors.

SAVORY EGG AND VEGETABLE BOWL

Prep Time: 10 minutes Cook Time: 15 minutes Serves: 2

4 large eggs

2 tablespoons extra virgin olive oil

1 small zucchini, diced

1 red bell pepper, diced

1/2 red onion, diced

2 cloves garlic, minced

1 cup cherry tomatoes, halved

1/4 cup fresh basil, chopped

2 tablespoons nutritional yeast

1 tablespoon balsamic vinegar

1/4 cup olives, pitted and sliced

Sea salt and black pepper to taste

Heat 1 tablespoon olive oil in large skillet over medium heat. Add diced zucchini, bell pepper, and red onion, cooking for 6-8 minutes until vegetables are tender and lightly caramelized. Add minced garlic and cook for additional minute until fragrant. Add cherry tomatoes and cook for 2-3 minutes until they begin to soften. Season with sea salt and black pepper. In separate skillet, heat remaining olive oil and fry eggs to desired doneness. Divide sautéed vegetables between bowls and top each with two fried eggs. Sprinkle with fresh basil, nutritional yeast, and sliced olives. Drizzle with balsamic vinegar before serving. The combination provides complete protein with anti-inflammatory vegetables for sustained morning energy.

WARMING GOLDEN MILK BOWL

Prep Time: 5 minutes Cook Time: 8 minutes Serves: 2

1 cup rolled oats

1 1/2 cups coconut milk

1 tablespoon fresh turmeric root, grated

1 teaspoon fresh ginger root, grated

1/2 teaspoon ground cinnamon

1/4 teaspoon ground cardamom

1/4 teaspoon black pepper

2 tablespoons raw honey

2 tablespoons cashews, chopped

1 tablespoon coconut flakes

1 tablespoon golden raisins

Pinch of sea salt

Combine rolled oats with coconut milk in medium saucepan over medium heat. Add grated turmeric, ginger, cinnamon, cardamom, black pepper, and sea salt. Bring mixture to gentle boil, then reduce heat to low and simmer for 5-6 minutes, stirring frequently, until oats reach desired consistency. Remove from heat and stir in honey until dissolved completely. Divide between serving bowls and top with chopped cashews, coconut flakes, and golden raisins. Allow to cool slightly before serving to prevent burning while maintaining warming properties. The golden milk spices provide powerful anti-inflammatory compounds while creating deeply satisfying and comforting breakfast experience.

Healing Soups and Broths

Golden Bone Broth with Turmeric and Ginger

Prep Time: 30 minutes Cook Time: 12-24 hours Serves: 8

3-4 lbs grass-fed beef bones (mix of marrow and knuckle bones)

2 tablespoons apple cider vinegar

1 large onion, quartered

3 carrots, roughly chopped

3 celery stalks, roughly chopped

6 cloves garlic, smashed

2 inches fresh turmeric root, sliced

2 inches fresh ginger root, sliced

1 bunch fresh parsley stems

2 bay leaves

1 teaspoon black peppercorns

2 tablespoons sea salt

12-14 cups filtered water

Preheat oven to 425°F. Place bones on rimmed baking sheet and roast for 30 minutes, turning once halfway through to ensure even browning. Transfer roasted bones to large slow cooker or stockpot. Add apple cider vinegar and let sit for 30 minutes to help extract minerals from bones. Add onion, carrots, celery, garlic, turmeric, ginger, parsley stems, bay leaves, and peppercorns. Cover with filtered water by 2 inches. If using slow cooker, cook on low for 12-24 hours. If using stovetop, bring to gentle boil, then reduce to lowest simmer and cook 12-24 hours. Skim foam occasionally during first 2 hours. Add sea salt during final hour of cooking. Strain through fine mesh strainer, pressing vegetables to extract liquid. Cool completely before refrigerating. Remove fat layer once solidified. Store refrigerated for up to 5 days or freeze for up to 6 months. Reheat gently and consume 1 cup daily for maximum therapeutic benefit.

VEGETABLE MISO SOUP

Prep Time: 15 minutes Cook Time: 20 minutes Serves: 4

4 cups vegetable broth (low-sodium)

2 tablespoons white miso paste

1 tablespoon red miso paste

1 sheet kombu seaweed

1 cup shiitake mushrooms, sliced

1/2 cup firm tofu, cubed

2 green onions, sliced thin

1 cup baby spinach leaves

1 tablespoon fresh ginger, grated

2 cloves garlic, minced

1 tablespoon sesame oil

1 teaspoon rice vinegar

1/4 teaspoon white pepper

1 tablespoon wakame seaweed, soaked

Soak wakame seaweed in warm water for 10 minutes until softened, then drain and chop roughly. Heat sesame oil in large saucepan over medium heat. Add ginger and garlic, sauté for 1 minute until fragrant. Add shiitake mushrooms and cook for 3 minutes until softened. Add vegetable broth and kombu seaweed. Bring to gentle simmer and cook for 10 minutes. Remove kombu and discard. In small bowl, whisk miso pastes with 1/4 cup of hot broth until smooth and lump-free. Remove soup from heat and slowly whisk in miso mixture to prevent curdling. Add tofu, wakame, and spinach. Let sit for 2 minutes until spinach wilts. Stir in rice vinegar and white pepper. Garnish with green onions and serve immediately. Do not boil after adding miso to preserve beneficial probiotics. Consume warm but not scalding hot to maintain therapeutic properties.

Ginger-Garlic Immune Support Broth

Prep Time: 10 minutes Cook Time: 45 minutes Serves: 6

8 cups filtered water

1 whole organic chicken carcass (or 2 lbs chicken bones)

4 inches fresh ginger root, sliced thick

1 whole head garlic, halved crosswise

1 large onion, quartered

2 tablespoons coconut oil

1 tablespoon raw apple cider vinegar

1 teaspoon whole peppercorns

4 whole cloves

1 cinnamon stick

2 star anise pods

1 tablespoon sea salt

2 tablespoons fresh lemon juice

Fresh cilantro for garnish

Heat coconut oil in large stockpot over medium-high heat. Add chicken bones and brown on all sides, about 8 minutes total. Add ginger, garlic, and onion. Sauté for 5 minutes until vegetables begin to caramelize. Add apple cider vinegar and let sit for 5 minutes to help extract minerals. Add filtered water, peppercorns, cloves, cinnamon stick, and star anise. Bring to gentle boil, then reduce heat to maintain low simmer. Skim any foam that rises to surface during first hour. Simmer partially covered for 3-4 hours, adding water as needed to maintain liquid level. Add sea salt during final 30 minutes of cooking. Strain through fine mesh strainer, pressing solids to extract maximum liquid. Discard solids. Stir in fresh lemon juice just before serving. Garnish with fresh cilantro. Consume 1 cup warm broth 2-3 times daily during illness or times of high stress. Store refrigerated for up to 4 days or freeze for up to 3 months.

TURMERIC LENTIL HEALING SOUP

Prep Time: 20 minutes Cook Time: 35 minutes Serves: 6

1 cup red lentils, rinsed

3 cups vegetable broth

1 can (14 oz) coconut milk (full-fat)

1 large onion, diced

3 carrots, diced

2 celery stalks, diced

4 cloves garlic, minced

2 inches fresh turmeric root, grated

1 inch fresh ginger root, grated

2 tablespoons coconut oil

1 teaspoon ground cumin

1 teaspoon ground coriander

1/2 teaspoon ground cardamom

1/4 teaspoon black pepper

1 teaspoon sea salt

2 cups fresh spinach, chopped

Juice of 1 lemon

Fresh cilantro for garnish

Heat coconut oil in large Dutch oven over medium heat. Add onion, carrots, and celery. Cook for 8 minutes until vegetables begin to soften. Add garlic, fresh turmeric, ginger, cumin, coriander, and cardamom. Cook for 2 minutes until spices become fragrant. Add red lentils and stir to coat with spice mixture. Pour in vegetable broth and bring to boil. Reduce heat to simmer, cover partially, and cook for 20 minutes until lentils are tender and breaking apart. Stir in coconut milk, black pepper, and sea salt. Simmer additional 5 minutes to blend flavors. Remove from heat and stir in chopped spinach until wilted. Add lemon juice and adjust seasoning to taste. For smoother texture, blend portion of soup with immersion blender, leaving some chunks for texture. Garnish with fresh cilantro and serve warm. This soup improves in flavor overnight and can be stored refrigerated for up to 5 days. Thin with additional broth when reheating if needed.

MUSHROOM-MISO ADAPTOGENIC BROTH

Prep Time: 25 minutes Cook Time: 1 hour Serves: 4

6 cups filtered water

1 oz dried shiitake mushrooms

1 oz dried reishi mushrooms

1/2 oz dried maitake mushrooms

2 tablespoons white miso paste

1 tablespoon red miso paste

2 inches fresh ginger, sliced

4 cloves garlic, smashed

1 sheet kombu seaweed

1 bunch green onions, chopped (whites and greens separated)

1 tablespoon sesame oil

1 teaspoon rice vinegar

1/4 teaspoon white pepper

1 tablespoon coconut aminos

Fresh chives for garnish

Rinse dried mushrooms under cold water to remove any debris. Place mushrooms in large bowl and cover with 4 cups warm water. Soak for 30 minutes until softened. Reserve soaking liquid and strain through fine mesh strainer lined with cheesecloth to remove any grit. Roughly chop rehydrated mushrooms, removing any tough stems. Heat sesame oil in large stockpot over medium heat. Add white parts of green onions, ginger, and garlic. Sauté for 3 minutes until fragrant. Add chopped mushrooms and cook for 5 minutes until they release their liquid. Add mushroom soaking liquid, additional filtered water, and kombu seaweed. Bring to gentle boil, then reduce to simmer. Cook for 45 minutes partially covered. Remove kombu and discard. In small bowl, whisk both miso pastes with 1/2 cup of hot broth until smooth. Remove soup from heat and slowly whisk in miso mixture. Stir in rice vinegar, white pepper, and coconut aminos. Garnish with green parts of scallions and fresh chives. Consume 1 cup daily to support immune function and stress resilience. Store refrigerated for up to 4 days.

Healing Chicken and Vegetable Soup

Prep Time: 30 minutes Cook Time: 1 hour 15 minutes Serves: 8

1 whole organic chicken (3-4 lbs)

10 cups filtered water

2 tablespoons apple cider vinegar

2 large onions, diced

4 carrots, sliced

4 celery stalks, sliced

1 parsnip, diced

6 cloves garlic, minced

2 inches fresh ginger, grated

2 bay leaves

1 bunch fresh parsley

1 bunch fresh dill

2 teaspoons sea salt

1/2 teaspoon black pepper

2 cups cooked wild rice

Juice of 1 lemon

Place whole chicken in large stockpot and cover with filtered water. Add apple cider vinegar and let sit for 30 minutes to help extract minerals. Add half of the onions, carrots, celery, garlic, ginger, bay leaves, and herb stems (reserve herb leaves for later). Bring to gentle boil, then reduce heat to maintain low simmer. Cook for 1 hour, skimming foam occasionally. Remove chicken carefully and set aside to cool. Strain broth through fine mesh strainer and return to pot. When chicken is cool enough to handle, remove and shred meat, discarding skin and bones. Return shredded chicken to strained broth. Add remaining vegetables and bring to simmer. Cook for 15 minutes until vegetables are tender. Stir in cooked wild rice, chopped herb leaves, sea salt, and black pepper. Simmer additional 5 minutes to heat through. Remove from heat and stir in lemon juice. Adjust seasoning to taste. Serve hot and consume within 30 minutes of preparation for maximum therapeutic benefit. Store refrigerated for up to 4 days or freeze for up to 3 months.

Gut-Healing Cabbage and Ginger Soup

Prep Time: 15 minutes Cook Time: 30 minutes Serves: 6

1 medium head green cabbage, chopped

6 cups vegetable broth

1 large onion, diced

3 inches fresh ginger root, grated

4 cloves garlic, minced

2 tablespoons coconut oil

1 tablespoon raw apple cider vinegar

1 teaspoon caraway seeds

1 teaspoon sea salt

1/4 teaspoon black pepper

2 tablespoons fresh lemon juice

1/4 cup fresh parsley, chopped

2 tablespoons raw sauerkraut (for serving)

Heat coconut oil in large Dutch oven over medium heat. Add onion and cook for 5 minutes until softened and translucent. Add grated ginger, garlic, and caraway seeds. Cook for 2 minutes until fragrant, stirring constantly to prevent burning. Add chopped cabbage and stir to coat with aromatics. Cook for 5 minutes until cabbage begins to wilt and release moisture. Pour in vegetable broth and apple cider vinegar. Bring to boil, then reduce heat to simmer. Cover and cook for 20 minutes until cabbage is very tender. Season with sea salt and black pepper. Remove from heat and stir in lemon juice and fresh parsley. For smoother texture, blend half the soup with immersion blender, leaving remaining soup chunky. Serve hot and top each bowl with 1 tablespoon raw sauerkraut for additional probiotic benefit. This soup is particularly beneficial for digestive healing when consumed warm but not scalding. Store refrigerated for up to 5 days. Flavor improves with time as ingredients meld together.

Beet and Ginger Borscht

Prep Time: 20 minutes Cook Time: 45 minutes Serves: 6

4 large beets, peeled and diced

6 cups vegetable broth

1 large onion, diced

2 carrots, diced

2 celery stalks, diced

3 inches fresh ginger root, grated

4 cloves garlic, minced

2 tablespoons coconut oil

2 tablespoons raw apple cider vinegar

1 can (14 oz) coconut milk

1 teaspoon ground cumin

1/2 teaspoon ground cardamom

1 teaspoon sea salt

1/4 teaspoon black pepper

2 tablespoons fresh dill, chopped

Coconut yogurt for serving

Heat coconut oil in large Dutch oven over medium heat. Add onion, carrots, and celery. Cook for 8 minutes until vegetables begin to soften. Add grated ginger, garlic, cumin, and cardamom. Cook for 2 minutes until spices become fragrant. Add diced beets and stir to coat with spice mixture. Cook for 5 minutes, stirring occasionally. Pour in vegetable broth and apple cider vinegar. Bring to boil, then reduce heat to simmer. Cover and cook for 30 minutes until beets are fork-tender. Stir in coconut milk and simmer additional 5 minutes. Season with sea salt and black pepper. For smoother consistency, blend half the soup with immersion blender, or blend entirely for completely smooth texture. Remove from heat and stir in fresh dill. Serve hot with dollop of coconut yogurt. This deeply pigmented soup provides powerful antioxidants and anti-inflammatory compounds. The natural nitrates in beets support circulation and cardiovascular health. Store refrigerated for up to 5 days. Color may deepen over time, which is normal.

HEALING FISH AND FENNEL BROTH

Prep Time: 25 minutes Cook Time: 40 minutes Serves: 4

1 lb wild-caught white fish fillets (cod or halibut)

6 cups fish stock or vegetable broth

2 fennel bulbs, sliced thin (reserve fronds)

1 large onion, sliced

3 cloves garlic, minced

2 inches fresh ginger, grated

2 tablespoons olive oil

1 tablespoon raw apple cider vinegar

1 teaspoon ground turmeric

1/2 teaspoon ground coriander

1/4 teaspoon saffron threads

1 teaspoon sea salt

1/4 teaspoon white pepper

Juice of 1 lemon

Fresh fennel fronds for garnish

Heat olive oil in large Dutch oven over medium heat. Add sliced onion and fennel bulbs. Cook for 10 minutes until vegetables begin to caramelize and soften. Add garlic, ginger, turmeric, coriander, and saffron. Cook for 2 minutes until spices become fragrant and saffron releases its color. Pour in fish stock and apple cider vinegar. Bring to gentle simmer and cook for 20 minutes to allow flavors to meld. Season fish fillets with sea salt and white pepper. Gently add fish to simmering broth and cook for 8-10 minutes until fish flakes easily with fork. Do not overcook fish. Remove fish carefully and flake into large pieces, removing any bones. Return flaked fish to broth and remove from heat immediately. Stir in lemon juice and adjust seasoning to taste. Garnish with reserved fennel fronds and serve immediately. This light, digestible soup provides omega-3 fatty acids and easily absorbed protein. Particularly beneficial during recovery from illness or digestive distress. Best consumed fresh and should not be stored longer than 2 days refrigerated.

Spiced Sweet Potato and Coconut Soup

Prep Time: 20 minutes Cook Time: 35 minutes Serves: 6

3 large sweet potatoes, peeled and cubed

1 can (14 oz) coconut milk (full-fat)

4 cups vegetable broth

1 large onion, diced

3 cloves garlic, minced

2 inches fresh ginger, grated

2 tablespoons coconut oil

1 teaspoon ground cinnamon

1/2 teaspoon ground nutmeg

1/4 teaspoon ground cloves

1/4 teaspoon cayenne pepper

1 teaspoon sea salt

1/4 teaspoon black pepper

2 tablespoons raw honey

Juice of 1 lime

1/4 cup pumpkin seeds, toasted

Fresh cilantro for garnish

Heat coconut oil in large Dutch oven over medium heat. Add diced onion and cook for 6 minutes until softened and lightly golden. Add garlic, ginger, cinnamon, nutmeg, cloves, and cayenne. Cook for 2 minutes until spices become fragrant, stirring constantly to prevent burning. Add cubed sweet potatoes and stir to coat with spice mixture. Cook for 5 minutes, stirring occasionally. Pour in vegetable broth and bring to boil. Reduce heat to simmer, cover, and cook for 20 minutes until sweet potatoes are very tender and easily pierced with fork. Remove from heat and blend until completely smooth using immersion blender or regular blender in batches. Return to pot if using regular blender. Stir in coconut milk, sea salt, black pepper, and honey. Simmer gently for 5 minutes to blend flavors. Remove from heat and stir in lime juice. Adjust seasoning to taste, adding more honey for sweetness or lime juice for brightness. Serve hot garnished with toasted pumpkin seeds and fresh cilantro. This creamy, naturally sweet soup provides beta-carotene and anti-inflammatory compounds. Store refrigerated for up to 5 days. Thin with additional broth when reheating if needed.

Fermented Foods and Probiotic Preparations

TURMERIC KRAUT

Prep Time: 30 minutes Fermentation Time: 7-14 days Serves: 8

2 lbs organic green cabbage, shredded

1 tablespoon fresh turmeric root, grated (or 1 teaspoon ground)

1 inch fresh ginger root, grated

2 cloves garlic, minced

1 tablespoon sea salt

1 teaspoon caraway seeds

1/2 teaspoon black pepper

1 bay leaf

1 tablespoon whey from yogurt (optional)

Remove outer leaves from cabbage and set aside 2-3 clean leaves for later use. Shred remaining cabbage finely using knife or food processor. Place shredded cabbage in large mixing bowl and sprinkle with sea salt. Massage cabbage vigorously with clean hands for 5-10 minutes until liquid begins to release and cabbage becomes wilted. Add grated turmeric, ginger, minced garlic, caraway seeds, and black pepper. Mix thoroughly until evenly distributed. Add whey if using for faster fermentation. Pack mixture tightly into clean quart jar, pressing down firmly to release more liquid. Liquid should cover vegetables by at least 1 inch. If insufficient liquid, add 2% salt brine (1 teaspoon salt per cup water). Place reserved cabbage leaf on top to keep vegetables submerged. Cover with loose lid or fermentation weight. Ferment at room temperature for 7-14 days, tasting daily after day 5. Refrigerate when desired tanginess is reached. Use within 6 months.

GINGER-CARROT KVASS DIGESTIVE TONIC

Prep Time: 20 minutes Fermentation Time: 3-5 days Serves: 6

4 large organic carrots, chopped into 1-inch pieces

2 inches fresh ginger root, sliced

1 tablespoon sea salt

2 tablespoons whey from yogurt (or additional 1 teaspoon salt)

4 cups filtered water

1 tablespoon raw honey

1 bay leaf

1/2 teaspoon whole coriander seeds

Wash and chop carrots into uniform pieces, leaving skin on for additional beneficial bacteria. Place chopped carrots and sliced ginger in clean half-gallon jar. Dissolve sea salt in 1 cup warm filtered water, stirring until completely dissolved. Add honey to salt water and stir until dissolved. Add remaining 3 cups filtered water, whey, bay leaf, and coriander seeds. Pour liquid over vegetables, ensuring they are completely covered by at least 2 inches. If needed, add more 2% salt brine. Weight vegetables down with fermentation weight or clean stone wrapped in cheesecloth. Cover jar with loose lid or cloth secured with rubber band. Ferment at room temperature for 3-5 days, tasting daily after day 2. Liquid should become slightly fizzy and develop tangy, earthy flavor. Strain liquid through fine mesh strainer, reserving both liquid and vegetables. Store strained kvass in refrigerator and consume 1/4 cup before meals for digestive support. Fermented vegetables can be eaten as condiment. Use within 1 month.

PROBIOTIC COCONUT YOGURT

Prep Time: 15 minutes Culturing Time: 12-24 hours Serves: 4

2 cans (14 oz each) full-fat coconut milk, chilled overnight

2 tablespoons grass-fed gelatin powder

1/4 cup warm filtered water

2 probiotic capsules (50+ billion CFU) or 2 tablespoons live yogurt starter

1 tablespoon raw honey (optional)

1 teaspoon vanilla extract (optional)

Chill coconut milk cans in refrigerator overnight to allow cream to separate. Open cans and scoop out thick cream, reserving liquid for other uses. Sprinkle gelatin over warm filtered water and let bloom for 5 minutes until absorbed. Heat 1/2 cup of coconut cream gently until just warm (not hot). Whisk bloomed gelatin into warm coconut cream until completely dissolved. Add remaining coconut cream and whisk until smooth. Allow mixture to cool to room temperature (important: too hot will kill probiotics). Open probiotic capsules and sprinkle contents into cooled coconut mixture, or add yogurt starter. Whisk thoroughly to distribute probiotics evenly. Add honey and vanilla if using. Pour mixture into clean glass jars, leaving 1 inch headspace. Cover with loose lids or cheesecloth. Place in yogurt maker, dehydrator set to 110°F, or oven with light on for 12-24 hours. Check after 12 hours - yogurt should be thick and tangy. Refrigerate immediately once desired flavor is reached. Consume within 1 week for maximum probiotic benefit.

FERMENTED SALSA VERDE

Prep Time: 25 minutes Fermentation Time: 3-5 days Serves: 6

2 lbs tomatillos, husked and quartered

1 white onion, diced

2 jalapeños, seeded and minced

4 cloves garlic, minced

1/4 cup fresh cilantro, chopped

2 tablespoons sea salt

1 tablespoon whey from yogurt (or additional 1 teaspoon salt)

Juice of 1 lime

1 teaspoon ground cumin

1/2 teaspoon dried oregano

Remove husks from tomatillos and rinse under cold water to remove sticky residue. Quarter tomatillos and place in large mixing bowl. Add diced onion, minced jalapeños, garlic, and chopped cilantro. Sprinkle vegetables with sea salt and massage vigorously for 5 minutes until juices begin to release. Add whey, lime juice, cumin, and oregano. Mix thoroughly until all ingredients are well combined. Pack mixture tightly into clean quart jar, pressing down firmly to release additional liquid. Liquid should cover vegetables by at least 1 inch. If insufficient liquid, add 2% salt brine as needed. Place fermentation weight on top to keep vegetables submerged. Cover with loose lid or cloth secured with rubber band. Ferment at room temperature for 3-5 days, checking daily and pressing down vegetables if they rise above liquid. Taste after day 3 - salsa should develop tangy, complex flavor. Refrigerate when desired taste is achieved. Use as condiment or dip. Consume within 2 months for best quality.

TRADITIONAL WATER KEFIR

Prep Time: 10 minutes Fermentation Time: 24-48 hours Serves: 4

1/4 cup water kefir grains

4 cups filtered water (non-chlorinated)

1/4 cup organic cane sugar

1/4 teaspoon sea salt

1/2 organic lemon, juiced

2 organic dried figs or dates

1 slice organic lemon with peel

Dissolve sugar and sea salt in filtered water, stirring until completely dissolved. Allow to cool to room temperature if heated. Place water kefir grains in clean quart jar. Pour sugar water over grains, ensuring they are completely covered. Add lemon juice, dried fruit, and lemon slice to provide additional minerals for fermentation. Cover jar with tight-fitting lid for first fermentation. Ferment at room temperature for 24-48 hours. Shorter fermentation produces sweeter kefir, longer fermentation creates more tart, probiotic-rich beverage. Strain kefir through plastic strainer (avoid metal), reserving grains for next batch. Remove fruit and lemon slice. For second fermentation (optional): pour strained kefir into swing-top bottles, leaving 1 inch headspace. Add desired flavorings such as fresh fruit, herbs, or ginger. Seal tightly and ferment additional 12-24 hours for carbonation. Refrigerate and consume within 1 week. Store grains in sugar water in refrigerator between batches.

CULTURED CASHEW CHEESE

Prep Time: 20 minutes Soaking Time: 4 hours Culturing Time: 24-48 hours Serves: 6

2 cups raw cashews, soaked 4 hours

1/2 cup filtered water

2 probiotic capsules (50+ billion CFU)

1 teaspoon sea salt

1 tablespoon nutritional yeast

1 tablespoon lemon juice

1 clove garlic, minced

1 tablespoon fresh herbs (thyme, rosemary, or chives)

1/4 teaspoon white pepper

Soak cashews in filtered water for 4 hours or overnight until softened. Drain and rinse thoroughly. Place soaked cashews and 1/2 cup fresh filtered water in high-speed blender. Blend on high speed for 2-3 minutes until completely smooth and creamy, scraping sides as needed. Open probiotic capsules and sprinkle contents into cashew mixture. Add sea salt and blend briefly to incorporate probiotics evenly. Transfer mixture to clean glass bowl and cover with cheesecloth or clean kitchen towel. Secure with rubber band and place in warm location (70-75°F) for 24-48 hours to culture. Mixture should develop tangy flavor and slightly thicker consistency. After culturing, add nutritional yeast, lemon juice, minced garlic, fresh herbs, and white pepper. Mix thoroughly until well combined. Taste and adjust seasoning as needed. Transfer to clean container and refrigerate. Cheese will continue to develop flavor and firm up in refrigerator. Use within 1 week as spread, dip, or cooking ingredient.

FERMENTED HOT SAUCE

Prep Time: 35 minutes Fermentation Time: 1-4 weeks Serves: 8

1 lb mixed hot peppers (jalapeño, serrano, habanero), stems removed

4 cloves garlic, peeled

1 small onion, quartered

2 tablespoons sea salt

1 tablespoon whey from yogurt (optional)

1 tablespoon raw apple cider vinegar

1 teaspoon raw honey

1/2 teaspoon ground cumin

Wear gloves when handling hot peppers to prevent skin irritation. Remove stems from peppers but leave seeds for maximum heat and beneficial bacteria. Roughly chop peppers, garlic, and onion into uniform pieces. Place chopped vegetables in food processor and pulse until coarsely chopped but not pureed. Transfer chopped mixture to large mixing bowl and sprinkle with sea salt. Massage vegetables for 3-5 minutes until juices begin to release. Add whey if using for faster fermentation startup. Pack mixture tightly into clean pint jar, pressing down to release more liquid. Liquid should cover vegetables by 1/2 inch minimum. Add 2% salt brine if needed to cover completely. Place fermentation weight on top to keep vegetables submerged. Cover with loose lid or cloth. Ferment at room temperature for 1-4 weeks, tasting weekly to monitor flavor development. Longer fermentation creates more complex, less harsh heat. When desired flavor is reached, blend fermented mixture until smooth. Add apple cider vinegar, honey, and cumin. Blend until well combined. Strain through fine mesh if smooth sauce is desired. Store in refrigerator in glass bottles. Use within 6 months for best quality and probiotic benefits.

PROBIOTIC BEET KVASS

Prep Time: 15 minutes Fermentation Time: 5-7 days Serves: 8

3 medium organic beets, scrubbed and cubed

1 tablespoon sea salt

2 tablespoons whey from yogurt (or additional 1 teaspoon salt)

Filtered water to cover

1 bay leaf

3 whole peppercorns

1 slice organic lemon with peel

Scrub beets thoroughly under running water but do not peel, as beneficial bacteria live on the skin. Cut beets into 1-inch cubes and place in clean half-gallon jar. Add sea salt, whey, bay leaf, peppercorns, and lemon slice. Fill jar with filtered water, leaving 2 inches headspace at top. Stir gently to dissolve salt completely. Cover vegetables with fermentation weight to keep submerged. Cover jar with loose lid or cheesecloth secured with rubber band. Ferment at room temperature for 5-7 days, checking daily to ensure vegetables remain submerged. Kvass should develop deep red color and earthy, slightly salty flavor with mild fermentation tang. Taste daily after day 4 to monitor flavor development. When desired taste is achieved, strain liquid through fine mesh strainer into clean bottles. Reserve fermented beets for second batch by adding fresh water and fermenting additional 3-5 days. Store finished kvass in refrigerator and consume 1/4 cup daily as digestive tonic. Use within 1 month for maximum probiotic benefit.

FERMENTED GARLIC HONEY

Prep Time: 10 minutes Fermentation Time: 1-2 weeks Serves: 20

1 cup organic garlic cloves, peeled

1/2 cup raw, unfiltered honey

1/4 teaspoon sea salt

1 bay leaf

3 whole peppercorns

Select firm, fresh garlic cloves without green shoots or soft spots. Peel cloves completely, removing any papery skin. Lightly crush each clove with flat side of knife to release juices and create surface area for fermentation. Place crushed garlic cloves in clean 8-ounce jar. Add sea salt, bay leaf, and peppercorns. Pour raw honey over garlic, stirring gently with clean wooden spoon to coat all cloves and dissolve salt. Garlic should be completely covered by honey. If needed, add additional honey to cover. Place clean fermentation weight on top to keep garlic submerged in honey. Cover jar with loose lid or cheesecloth secured with rubber band. Ferment at room temperature for 1-2 weeks, stirring gently every 2-3 days with clean wooden spoon. Fermentation creates bubbles and slightly thins honey consistency. Taste after 1 week - garlic should become milder and honey should develop complex, savory notes. Ferment longer for stronger flavor development. Store at room temperature or refrigerate for longer storage. Consume 1 teaspoon daily during illness or as immune support. Use within 6 months for best quality.

CULTURED BUTTER AND BUTTERMILK

Prep Time: 20 minutes Culturing Time: 12-24 hours Churning Time: 15 minutes Serves: 4

2 cups heavy cream (preferably grass-fed, non-homogenized)

1/4 cup cultured buttermilk or 1 packet butter culture

1/4 teaspoon sea salt (optional)

Ice water for washing

Ensure cream is at room temperature before beginning. Pour cream into clean glass jar and add cultured buttermilk or butter culture. Stir gently with clean wooden spoon to distribute culture evenly. Cover jar with loose lid or cheesecloth and allow to culture at room temperature for 12-24 hours until cream thickens and develops tangy flavor. Cultured cream should coat spoon and taste pleasantly sour. Chill cultured cream in refrigerator for at least 2 hours before churning. Pour chilled cultured cream into food processor or stand mixer bowl. Process or whip on medium speed until cream thickens, then increases speed to high. Continue processing until cream separates into butter solids and liquid buttermilk, approximately 5-10 minutes total. Strain through fine mesh strainer, reserving both butter and buttermilk. Rinse butter solids under ice-cold water, pressing with wooden spoon until water runs clear. This removes excess buttermilk and prevents rancidity. Work salt into butter if desired. Press butter into clean container, removing any remaining liquid. Store cultured butter refrigerated for up to 2 weeks. Reserve cultured buttermilk for drinking, baking, or starting next batch. Buttermilk keeps refrigerated for 1 week and provides excellent probiotic benefits.

Snacks and Treats

GOLDEN TURMERIC ENERGY BALLS

Prep Time: 15 minutes Chill Time: 30 minutes Serves: 12 balls

1 cup pitted Medjool dates, soaked for 10 minutes

1/2 cup raw cashews

1/4 cup coconut flour

2 tablespoons almond butter

1 tablespoon coconut oil, melted

1 teaspoon ground turmeric

1/2 teaspoon ground ginger

1/4 teaspoon black pepper

1/4 teaspoon ground cinnamon

Pinch of sea salt

2 tablespoons unsweetened coconut flakes for rolling

Soak dates in warm water for 10 minutes to soften. Drain thoroughly and pat dry with paper towels. Process cashews in food processor for 30 seconds until they form coarse meal. Add drained dates and process for 60 seconds until mixture forms sticky paste. Add coconut flour, almond butter, melted coconut oil, turmeric, ginger, black pepper, cinnamon, and sea salt. Process until mixture holds together when pressed. If too dry, add coconut oil 1 teaspoon at a time. If too wet, add coconut flour 1 tablespoon at a time. Roll mixture into 12 equal balls using clean hands. Roll each ball in coconut flakes to coat. Place on parchment-lined plate and refrigerate for 30 minutes until firm. Store in airtight container in refrigerator for up to 1 week.

Omega-3 Seed Crackers

Prep Time: 20 minutes Dehydration Time: 12 hours Serves: 8

1/2 cup ground flaxseeds

1/4 cup chia seeds

1/4 cup hemp hearts

1/4 cup pumpkin seeds, ground

1/4 cup sunflower seeds, ground

1 teaspoon garlic powder

1 teaspoon onion powder

1/2 teaspoon smoked paprika

1/2 teaspoon dried oregano

1/2 teaspoon sea salt

1/4 teaspoon black pepper

3/4 cup filtered water

2 tablespoons olive oil

Combine ground flaxseeds, chia seeds, hemp hearts, ground pumpkin seeds, and ground sunflower seeds in large mixing bowl. Add garlic powder, onion powder, smoked paprika, oregano, sea salt, and black pepper. Mix thoroughly to distribute spices evenly. In separate bowl, whisk together filtered water and olive oil. Pour liquid mixture over seed mixture and stir until well combined. Let stand for 15 minutes to allow seeds to absorb liquid and form gel-like consistency. Spread mixture evenly on dehydrator tray lined with non-stick sheet, creating rectangle approximately 1/8 inch thick. Score into desired cracker sizes using knife. Dehydrate at 115°F for 12 hours until completely dry and crispy. Alternatively, bake in oven at lowest temperature (170°F) with door slightly open for 6-8 hours. Store in airtight container for up to 2 weeks.

CHOCOLATE BARK

Prep Time: 25 minutes Chill Time: 2 hours Serves: 16 pieces

8 oz dark chocolate (85% cacao), chopped

2 tablespoons coconut oil

1/4 cup raw almonds, roughly chopped

1/4 cup dried goji berries

2 tablespoons cacao nibs

1 tablespoon hemp hearts

1 teaspoon ground ginger

1/2 teaspoon ground turmeric

1/4 teaspoon ground cinnamon

Pinch of cayenne pepper

Flaky sea salt for finishing

Line 8x8 inch pan with parchment paper, leaving overhang for easy removal. Melt chocolate and coconut oil in double boiler over simmering water, stirring constantly until smooth. Remove from heat and let cool for 5 minutes. Stir in ground ginger, turmeric, cinnamon, and cayenne pepper until evenly distributed. Pour melted chocolate mixture into prepared pan and spread evenly using offset spatula. Immediately sprinkle chopped almonds, goji berries, cacao nibs, and hemp hearts over surface, pressing gently to adhere. Finish with light sprinkle of flaky sea salt. Refrigerate for 2 hours until completely set. Remove from pan using parchment overhang and break into 16 irregular pieces. Store in airtight container in refrigerator for up to 2 weeks.

Spiced Sweet Potato Chips

Prep Time: 15 minutes Baking Time: 45 minutes Serves: 4

2 large sweet potatoes, scrubbed and dried

2 tablespoons avocado oil

1 teaspoon ground turmeric

1/2 teaspoon ground cumin

1/2 teaspoon smoked paprika

1/4 teaspoon ground ginger

1/4 teaspoon garlic powder

1/4 teaspoon onion powder

1/2 teaspoon sea salt

1/4 teaspoon black pepper

Pinch of cayenne pepper

Preheat oven to 400°F. Line two large baking sheets with parchment paper. Using mandoline slicer or sharp knife, slice sweet potatoes into 1/8-inch thick rounds. Pat slices completely dry with paper towels to remove excess moisture. In large bowl, toss sweet potato slices with avocado oil until evenly coated. In small bowl, combine turmeric, cumin, smoked paprika, ginger, garlic powder, onion powder, sea salt, black pepper, and cayenne pepper. Sprinkle spice mixture over oiled sweet potato slices and toss until evenly coated. Arrange slices in single layer on prepared baking sheets, ensuring they don't overlap. Bake for 20 minutes, then flip each slice and rotate pans. Continue baking for 15-25 minutes until edges are crispy and centers are tender. Cool completely on baking sheets before serving. Store in airtight container for up to 3 days.

COCONUT MATCHA FAT BOMBS

Prep Time: 20 minutes Chill Time: 1 hour Serves: 15 bombs

1/2 cup coconut oil, softened

1/4 cup coconut butter

2 tablespoons grass-fed ghee

2 tablespoons ceremonial grade matcha powder

2 tablespoons powdered monk fruit sweetener

1 teaspoon vanilla extract

1/4 teaspoon ground ginger

Pinch of sea salt

1/4 cup unsweetened coconut flakes

2 tablespoons chopped pistachios

Sift matcha powder through fine mesh strainer to remove lumps. In medium bowl, cream together softened coconut oil, coconut butter, and ghee using electric mixer until light and fluffy. Add sifted matcha powder, monk fruit sweetener, vanilla extract, ground ginger, and sea salt. Mix on low speed until evenly combined and mixture is smooth green color. Fold in coconut flakes and chopped pistachios by hand. Line mini muffin tin with paper liners or use silicone molds. Divide mixture evenly among 15 molds, filling each about 3/4 full. Refrigerate for 1 hour until completely firm. Remove from molds and store in airtight container in refrigerator for up to 2 weeks. Serve chilled and consume within 10 minutes of removing from refrigerator.

TRAIL MIX

Prep Time: 10 minutes Roasting Time: 15 minutes Serves: 8

1/2 cup raw walnuts, roughly chopped

1/2 cup raw almonds, roughly chopped

1/4 cup pumpkin seeds

1/4 cup sunflower seeds

2 tablespoons coconut oil, melted

1 teaspoon ground turmeric

1/2 teaspoon ground ginger

1/4 teaspoon ground cinnamon

1/4 teaspoon sea salt

1/4 cup dried tart cherries (unsweetened)

2 tablespoons cacao nibs

2 tablespoons coconut flakes

Preheat oven to 325°F. Line large baking sheet with parchment paper. In large bowl, combine chopped walnuts, almonds, pumpkin seeds, and sunflower seeds. Drizzle with melted coconut oil and toss until evenly coated. In small bowl, mix together turmeric, ginger, cinnamon, and sea salt. Sprinkle spice mixture over nuts and seeds, tossing until evenly distributed. Spread mixture in single layer on prepared baking sheet. Roast for 12-15 minutes, stirring once halfway through, until nuts are golden and fragrant. Remove from oven and cool completely on baking sheet. Once cooled, transfer to large bowl and add dried tart cherries, cacao nibs, and coconut flakes. Toss to combine evenly. Store in airtight container at room temperature for up to 2 weeks.

GINGER-TURMERIC GUMMIES

Prep Time: 15 minutes Cook Time: 5 minutes Chill Time: 2 hours Serves: 24 gummies

1 cup coconut water

1/4 cup raw honey

2 tablespoons fresh ginger juice (from 2 inches ginger root)

1 tablespoon fresh turmeric juice (or 1 teaspoon ground turmeric)

2 tablespoons fresh lemon juice

1/4 teaspoon black pepper

Pinch of sea salt

4 tablespoons grass-fed gelatin powder

1/4 cup cold water

Grate fresh ginger and turmeric roots using microplane grater. Press grated ginger through fine mesh strainer or cheesecloth to extract 2 tablespoons juice. Repeat with turmeric to extract 1 tablespoon juice. In small bowl, sprinkle gelatin powder over cold water and let bloom for 5 minutes. In small saucepan, heat coconut water over medium heat until steaming but not boiling. Remove from heat and whisk in honey until dissolved. Add fresh ginger juice, turmeric juice, lemon juice, black pepper, and sea salt. Whisk to combine. Add bloomed gelatin mixture and whisk vigorously until gelatin completely dissolves. Strain mixture through fine mesh strainer to remove any lumps. Pour into silicone gummy molds or ice cube trays. Refrigerate for 2 hours until completely set. Remove from molds and store in airtight container in refrigerator for up to 1 week.

SAVORY HERB AND SEED BITES

Prep Time: 20 minutes Baking Time: 25 minutes Serves: 20 bites

1 cup almond flour

1/4 cup ground flaxseeds

1/4 cup hemp hearts

2 tablespoons nutritional yeast

1 teaspoon dried basil

1 teaspoon dried oregano

1/2 teaspoon garlic powder

1/2 teaspoon onion powder

1/2 teaspoon sea salt

1/4 teaspoon black pepper

2 tablespoons olive oil

1 large egg, beaten

2 tablespoons water (if needed)

Preheat oven to 350°F. Line baking sheet with parchment paper. In large bowl, combine almond flour, ground flaxseeds, hemp hearts, nutritional yeast, basil, oregano, garlic powder, onion powder, sea salt, and black pepper. Mix thoroughly to distribute seasonings evenly. In small bowl, whisk together olive oil and beaten egg. Pour wet ingredients over dry ingredients and mix until dough forms. If mixture seems too dry, add water 1 tablespoon at a time until dough holds together when pressed. Roll dough into 20 small balls, each about 1 inch in diameter. Place on prepared baking sheet and flatten slightly with fork, creating crosshatch pattern on top. Bake for 20-25 minutes until golden brown and firm to touch. Cool on baking sheet for 5 minutes before transferring to wire rack. Store in airtight container for up to 1 week.

CINNAMON APPLE CHIPS

Prep Time: 15 minutes Dehydrating Time: 8 hours Serves: 4

4 medium organic apples (Honeycrisp or Gala)

2 tablespoons fresh lemon juice

1 teaspoon ground cinnamon

1/2 teaspoon ground ginger

1/4 teaspoon ground cardamom

1/4 teaspoon ground nutmeg

Pinch of sea salt

Wash and dry apples thoroughly. Using mandoline slicer or sharp knife, slice apples into 1/8-inch thick rounds, removing seeds but leaving skin on. In large bowl, toss apple slices with lemon juice to prevent browning. In small bowl, combine cinnamon, ginger, cardamom, nutmeg, and sea salt. Sprinkle spice mixture over apple slices and toss until evenly coated. Arrange apple slices in single layer on dehydrator trays, ensuring they don't overlap. Dehydrate at 135°F for 6-8 hours until apples are completely dry and crispy. Alternatively, arrange on parchment-lined baking sheets and bake in oven at 200°F for 2-3 hours, flipping once halfway through, until crispy. Cool completely before storing. Store in airtight container for up to 2 weeks.

PROBIOTIC COCONUT YOGURT PARFAIT CUPS

Prep Time: 25 minutes Chill Time: 4 hours Serves: 6 cups

2 cups full-fat coconut milk (chilled overnight)

2 probiotic capsules (50 billion CFU)

2 tablespoons raw honey

1 teaspoon vanilla extract

1/4 teaspoon ground cinnamon

1 cup mixed berries (blueberries, raspberries, blackberries)

1/2 cup chopped walnuts

1/4 cup hemp hearts

2 tablespoons chia seeds

1 tablespoon coconut flakes

Fresh mint leaves for garnish

Chill coconut milk can in refrigerator overnight. Open can and scoop out thick coconut cream, leaving watery liquid behind. Place coconut cream in bowl and whip with electric mixer until light and fluffy. Open probiotic capsules and sprinkle powder into whipped coconut cream. Add honey, vanilla extract, and cinnamon. Mix gently until just combined, being careful not to over-mix. In small bowl, combine mixed berries with 1 tablespoon honey and let macerate for 10 minutes. In another bowl, mix chopped walnuts, hemp hearts, chia seeds, and coconut flakes. Layer ingredients in 6 small glass jars or cups: start with layer of probiotic coconut cream, add layer of macerated berries, sprinkle with nut and seed mixture. Repeat layers until jars are full, ending with coconut cream on top. Refrigerate for at least 4 hours to allow flavors to meld and chia seeds to soften. Garnish with fresh mint leaves before serving.

30-Day Anti-Inflammatory Diet Meal Plan

How to Use This Meal Plan

Daily Structure:
- Morning: Start with an anti-inflammatory elixir or smoothie
- Breakfast: Nutrient-dense bowl
- Lunch: Healing soup or broth
- Dinner: Varies by week (repeat breakfast bowls, soups, or create your own combinations)
- Snacks: Choose 1-2 anti-inflammatory snacks throughout the day
- Fermented Foods: Include one serving daily for gut health

Week 1: Foundation Phase

Focus: Establishing anti-inflammatory habits

Day 1
- Morning Elixir: Golden Turmeric Smoothie (p. 59)
- Breakfast: Golden Turmeric Quinoa Power Bowl (p. 70)
- Lunch: Golden Bone Broth with Turmeric and Ginger (p. 86)
- Dinner: Omega-3 Chia Seed Pudding Bowl (p. 71)
- Snacks: Golden Turmeric Energy Balls (p. 108)
- Fermented Food: Turmeric Kraut (p. 97)

Day 2
- Morning Elixir: Green Powerhouse (p. 60)
- Breakfast: Green Goddess Avocado Bowl (p. 72)
- Lunch: Vegetable Miso Soup (p. 87)
- Dinner: Berry Yogurt Bowl (p. 73)
- Snacks: Omega-3 Seed Crackers (p. 109)
- Fermented Food: Probiotic Coconut Yogurt (p. 99)

Day 3
- Morning Elixir: Tart Cherry Anti-Pain Elixir (p. 61)
- Breakfast: Warming Ginger Oat Bowl (p. 74)
- Lunch: Ginger-Garlic Immune Support Broth (p. 88)
- Dinner: Protein-Packed Quinoa Breakfast Bowl (p. 75)
- Snacks: Chocolate Bark (p. 110)
- Fermented Food: Ginger-Carrot Kvass Digestive Tonic (p. 98)

Day 4
- Morning Elixir: Omega-3 Brain Boost Smoothie (p. 62)
- Breakfast: Mediterranean Herb Bowl (p. 76)
- Lunch: Turmeric Lentil Healing Soup (p. 89)
- Dinner: Coconut Curry Breakfast Bowl (p. 77)
- Snacks: Spiced Sweet Potato Chips (p. 111)
- Fermented Food: Fermented Salsa Verde (p. 100)

Day 5
- Morning Elixir: Ginger Digestive Fire Elixir (p. 63)
- Breakfast: Antioxidant Acai Bowl (p. 78)
- Lunch: Mushroom-Miso Adaptogenic Broth (p. 90)
- Dinner: Savory Mushroom and Herb Bowl (p. 79)
- Snacks: Coconut Matcha Fat Bombs (p. 112)
- Fermented Food: Traditional Water Kefir (p. 101)

Day 6
- Morning Elixir: Adaptogenic Stress-Relief Smoothie (p. 64)
- Breakfast: Warming Sweet Potato Hash Bowl (p. 80)
- Lunch: Healing Chicken and Vegetable Soup (p. 91)
- Dinner: Protein-Rich Lentil Bowl (p. 81)
- Snacks: Trail Mix (p. 113)
- Fermented Food: Cultured Cashew Cheese (p. 102)

Day 7
- Morning Elixir: Beet Liver Detox Elixir (p. 65)
- Breakfast: Spiced Apple Cinnamon Bowl (p. 82)
- Lunch: Gut-Healing Cabbage and Ginger Soup (p. 92)
- Dinner: Savory Egg and Vegetable Bowl (p. 83)
- Snacks: Ginger-Turmeric Gummies (p. 114)
- Fermented Food: Fermented Hot Sauce (p. 103)

Week 2: Building Momentum

Focus: Deepening anti-inflammatory benefits

Day 8
- Morning Elixir: Collagen Repair Smoothie (p. 66)
- Breakfast: Warming Golden Milk Bowl (p. 84)
- Lunch: Beet and Ginger Borscht (p. 93)
- Dinner: Golden Turmeric Quinoa Power Bowl (p. 70)
- Snacks: Savory Herb and Seed Bites (p. 115)
- Fermented Food: Probiotic Beet Kvass (p. 104)

Day 9
- Morning Elixir: Hibiscus Antioxidant Elixir (p. 67)
- Breakfast: Green Goddess Avocado Bowl (p. 72)
- Lunch: Healing Fish and Fennel Broth (p. 94)
- Dinner: Omega-3 Chia Seed Pudding Bowl (p. 71)
- Snacks: Probiotic Coconut Yogurt Parfait Cups (p. 117)
- Fermented Food: Fermented Garlic Honey (p. 105)

Day 10
- Morning Elixir: Matcha Green Tea Recovery Smoothie (p. 68)
- Breakfast: Berry Yogurt Bowl (p. 73)
- Lunch: Spiced Sweet Potato and Coconut Soup (p. 95)
- Dinner: Warming Ginger Oat Bowl (p. 74)
- Snacks: Golden Turmeric Energy Balls (p. 108)
- Fermented Food: Cultured Butter and Buttermilk (p. 106)

Day 11
- Morning Elixir: Golden Turmeric Smoothie (p. 59)
- Breakfast: Protein-Packed Quinoa Breakfast Bowl (p. 75)
- Lunch: Golden Bone Broth with Turmeric and Ginger (p. 86)
- Dinner: Mediterranean Herb Bowl (p. 76)
- Snacks: Omega-3 Seed Crackers (p. 109)
- Fermented Food: Turmeric Kraut (p. 97)

Day 12
- Morning Elixir: Green Powerhouse (p. 60)
- Breakfast: Coconut Curry Breakfast Bowl (p. 77)
- Lunch: Vegetable Miso Soup (p. 87)
- Dinner: Antioxidant Acai Bowl (p. 78)
- Snacks: Chocolate Bark (p. 110)
- Fermented Food: Ginger-Carrot Kvass Digestive Tonic (p. 98)

Day 13
- Morning Elixir: Tart Cherry Anti-Pain Elixir (p. 61)
- Breakfast: Savory Mushroom and Herb Bowl (p. 79)
- Lunch: Ginger-Garlic Immune Support Broth (p. 88)
- Dinner: Warming Sweet Potato Hash Bowl (p. 80)
- Snacks: Spiced Sweet Potato Chips (p. 111)
- Fermented Food: Probiotic Coconut Yogurt (p. 99)

Day 14
- Morning Elixir: Omega-3 Brain Boost Smoothie (p. 62)
- Breakfast: Protein-Rich Lentil Bowl (p. 81)
- Lunch: Turmeric Lentil Healing Soup (p. 89)
- Dinner: Spiced Apple Cinnamon Bowl (p. 82)
- Snacks: Coconut Matcha Fat Bombs (p. 112)
- Fermented Food: Fermented Salsa Verde (p. 100)

Week 3: Optimizing Results

Focus: Peak anti-inflammatory benefits

Day 15
- Morning Elixir: Ginger Digestive Fire Elixir (p. 63)
- Breakfast: Savory Egg and Vegetable Bowl (p. 83)
- Lunch: Mushroom-Miso Adaptogenic Broth (p. 90)
- Dinner: Warming Golden Milk Bowl (p. 84)
- Snacks: Trail Mix (p. 113)
- Fermented Food: Traditional Water Kefir (p. 101)

Day 16
- Morning Elixir: Adaptogenic Stress-Relief Smoothie (p. 64)
- Breakfast: Golden Turmeric Quinoa Power Bowl (p. 70)
- Lunch: Healing Chicken and Vegetable Soup (p. 91)
- Dinner: Green Goddess Avocado Bowl (p. 72)
- Snacks: Ginger-Turmeric Gummies (p. 114)

- Fermented Food: Cultured Cashew Cheese (p. 102)

Day 17
- Morning Elixir: Beet Liver Detox Elixir (p. 65)
- Breakfast: Omega-3 Chia Seed Pudding Bowl (p. 71)
- Lunch: Gut-Healing Cabbage and Ginger Soup (p. 92)
- Dinner: Berry Yogurt Bowl (p. 73)
- Snacks: Savory Herb and Seed Bites (p. 115)
- Fermented Food: Fermented Hot Sauce (p. 103)

Day 18
- Morning Elixir: Collagen Repair Smoothie (p. 66)
- Breakfast: Warming Ginger Oat Bowl (p. 74)
- Lunch: Beet and Ginger Borscht (p. 93)
- Dinner: Protein-Packed Quinoa Breakfast Bowl (p. 75)
- Snacks: Probiotic Coconut Yogurt Parfait Cups (p. 117)
- Fermented Food: Probiotic Beet Kvass (p. 104)

Day 19
- Morning Elixir: Hibiscus Antioxidant Elixir (p. 67)
- Breakfast: Mediterranean Herb Bowl (p. 76)
- Lunch: Healing Fish and Fennel Broth (p. 94)
- Dinner: Coconut Curry Breakfast Bowl (p. 77)
- Snacks: Golden Turmeric Energy Balls (p. 108)
- Fermented Food: Fermented Garlic Honey (p. 105)

Day 20
- Morning Elixir: Matcha Green Tea Recovery Smoothie (p. 68)
- Breakfast: Antioxidant Acai Bowl (p. 78)
- Lunch: Spiced Sweet Potato and Coconut Soup (p. 95)
- Dinner: Savory Mushroom and Herb Bowl (p. 79)
- Snacks: Omega-3 Seed Crackers (p. 109)
- Fermented Food: Cultured Butter and Buttermilk (p. 106)

Day 21
- Morning Elixir: Golden Turmeric Smoothie (p. 59)
- Breakfast: Warming Sweet Potato Hash Bowl (p. 80)
- Lunch: Golden Bone Broth with Turmeric and Ginger (p. 86)
- Dinner: Protein-Rich Lentil Bowl (p. 81)
- Snacks: Chocolate Bark (p. 110)
- Fermented Food: Turmeric Kraut (p. 97)

Week 4: Mastery and Maintenance

Focus: Establishing long-term habits

Day 22
- Morning Elixir: Green Powerhouse (p. 60)
- Breakfast: Spiced Apple Cinnamon Bowl (p. 82)
- Lunch: Vegetable Miso Soup (p. 87)
- Dinner: Savory Egg and Vegetable Bowl (p. 83)

- Snacks: Spiced Sweet Potato Chips (p. 111)
- Fermented Food: Ginger-Carrot Kvass Digestive Tonic (p. 98)

Day 23
- Morning Elixir: Tart Cherry Anti-Pain Elixir (p. 61)
- Breakfast: Warming Golden Milk Bowl (p. 84)
- Lunch: Ginger-Garlic Immune Support Broth (p. 88)
- Dinner: Golden Turmeric Quinoa Power Bowl (p. 70)
- Snacks: Coconut Matcha Fat Bombs (p. 112)
- Fermented Food: Probiotic Coconut Yogurt (p. 99)

Day 24
- Morning Elixir: Omega-3 Brain Boost Smoothie (p. 62)
- Breakfast: Green Goddess Avocado Bowl (p. 72)
- Lunch: Turmeric Lentil Healing Soup (p. 89)
- Dinner: Omega-3 Chia Seed Pudding Bowl (p. 71)
- Snacks: Trail Mix (p. 113)
- Fermented Food: Fermented Salsa Verde (p. 100)

Day 25
- Morning Elixir: Ginger Digestive Fire Elixir (p. 63)
- Breakfast: Berry Yogurt Bowl (p. 73)
- Lunch: Mushroom-Miso Adaptogenic Broth (p. 90)
- Dinner: Warming Ginger Oat Bowl (p. 74)
- Snacks: Ginger-Turmeric Gummies (p. 114)
- Fermented Food: Traditional Water Kefir (p. 101)

Day 26
- Morning Elixir: Adaptogenic Stress-Relief Smoothie (p. 64)
- Breakfast: Protein-Packed Quinoa Breakfast Bowl (p. 75)
- Lunch: Healing Chicken and Vegetable Soup (p. 91)
- Dinner: Mediterranean Herb Bowl (p. 76)
- Snacks: Savory Herb and Seed Bites (p. 115)
- Fermented Food: Cultured Cashew Cheese (p. 102)

Day 27
- Morning Elixir: Beet Liver Detox Elixir (p. 65)
- Breakfast: Coconut Curry Breakfast Bowl (p. 77)
- Lunch: Gut-Healing Cabbage and Ginger Soup (p. 92)
- Dinner: Antioxidant Acai Bowl (p. 78)
- Snacks: Probiotic Coconut Yogurt Parfait Cups (p. 117)
- Fermented Food: Fermented Hot Sauce (p. 103)

Day 28
- Morning Elixir: Collagen Repair Smoothie (p. 66)
- Breakfast: Savory Mushroom and Herb Bowl (p. 79)
- Lunch: Beet and Ginger Borscht (p. 93)
- Dinner: Warming Sweet Potato Hash Bowl (p. 80)
- Snacks: Golden Turmeric Energy Balls (p. 108)
- Fermented Food: Probiotic Beet Kvass (p. 104)

Day 29
- Morning Elixir: Hibiscus Antioxidant Elixir (p. 67)
- Breakfast: Protein-Rich Lentil Bowl (p. 81)
- Lunch: Healing Fish and Fennel Broth (p. 94)
- Dinner: Spiced Apple Cinnamon Bowl (p. 82)
- Snacks: Omega-3 Seed Crackers (p. 109)
- Fermented Food: Fermented Garlic Honey (p. 105)

Day 30
- Morning Elixir: Matcha Green Tea Recovery Smoothie (p. 68)
- Breakfast: Savory Egg and Vegetable Bowl (p. 83)
- Lunch: Spiced Sweet Potato and Coconut Soup (p. 95)
- Dinner: Warming Golden Milk Bowl (p. 84)
- Snacks: Chocolate Bark (p. 110)
- Fermented Food: Cultured Butter and Buttermilk (p. 106)

Printed in Dunstable, United Kingdom